Success in English Teaching

Also published in
Oxford Handbooks for Language Teachers

Teaching American English Pronunciation
Peter Avery and Susan Ehrlich

Teaching Business English
Mark Ellis and Christine Johnson

Teaching and Learning in the Language Classroom
Tricia Hedge

Teaching English Overseas: An Introduction
Sandra Lee McKay

How Languages are Learned (New Edition)
Patsy Lightbown and Nina Spada

Communication in the Language Classroom
Tony Lynch

Explaining English Grammar
George Yule

Success in English Teaching

Paul Davies

with Eric Pearse

OXFORD
UNIVERSITY PRESS

OXFORD
UNIVERSITY PRESS

Great Clarendon Street, Oxford OX2 6DP

Oxford University Press is a department of the University of Oxford.
It furthers the University's objective of excellence in research,
scholarship, and education by publishing worldwide in

Oxford New York

Athens Auckland Bangkok Bogotá Buenos Aires
Calcutta Cape Town Chennai Dar es Salaam Delhi Florence
Hong Kong Istanbul Karachi Kuala Lumpur Madrid Melbourne
Mexico City Mumbai Nairobi Paris São Paulo Singapore
Taipei Tokyo Toronto Warsaw

with associated companies in Berlin Ibadan

Oxford and Oxford English are registered trade marks of
Oxford University Press in the UK and in certain other countries

ISBN 0 19 442171 6

Printed in Hong Kong

For Emma and Hilda

CONTENTS

INTRODUCTION

Who is Success in English Teaching *for?*

This handbook is for anyone who is teaching or planning to teach English as a foreign language anywhere in the world. But it is especially for those who:

- are non-native speakers of English
- have little or no formal training as English teachers, or were trained some time ago
- are teaching in the students' own country, not an English-speaking country.

Most of these people will be teaching, or preparing to teach, English in an institution of general education—a school, college, or university. *Success in English Teaching* focuses especially on teaching at secondary-school level and above.

The book is also for teacher-trainers running both pre-service and in-service courses.

What does the book contain?

The twelve chapters which form the main body of the book cover every major aspect of teaching English. Chapters 1 to 7 focus on actual classroom teaching. They establish essential theoretical principles, and present a wide and coherent range of practical teaching ideas which are designed to be effective and acceptable in the working contexts of most teachers. Chapters 8 to 12 consider other aspects of teaching English: planning and management, materials and aids, evaluation and testing, and professional development, including a survey of past and current approaches. There are tasks and questions for discussion at appropriate points in the chapters. At the end of each chapter there is a summary of its contents and a project.

The book also contains a glossary, a list of sources and suggestions for further reading, and an index.

How can you make use of Success in English Teaching?

Like most books of its kind, *Success in English Teaching* can be used in several different ways. The main alternatives are to use it as:

– a complete course in English teaching
– a reference book.

The sequence of chapters is designed especially for people who wish to use the book as a complete course, working through it from beginning to end. The glossary can help with the understanding of new terms and concepts, and the projects at the end of each chapter can be made an integral part of the course. After completing the course, trainee teachers may wish to continue their development by selecting other books from the Sources and Further Reading section.

If you are a practising teacher, or a teacher-trainer, looking for new insights and ideas, you may just want to add *Success in English Teaching* to your personal reference library. In that case, you will find the contents pages and the index useful to locate the topic you are interested in at any given time. The summaries at the end of each chapter should also be useful, quickly providing more background to the topic you are investigating.

Whether you are a pre-service trainee, practising teacher, or teacher-trainer, we hope that you will find the book useful and interesting, and that it delivers the promise in its title.

PAUL DAVIES
ERIC PEARSE

1 A GENERAL APPROACH TO TEACHING ENGLISH

Introduction

In this chapter we define success in English language teaching and learning. That involves deciding on valid goals for English language courses. The development of an ability to communicate in English must be a major goal of any effective course. We present a general model of English language teaching (ELT) that integrates the use of English as the main classroom language from the start, appropriate focus on language, and regular communicative activities. For any approach to work, certain conditions are essential, such as dynamic lessons and motivation. Specific teaching–learning situations also have to be taken into account.

Recognizing success in teaching English

Many institutions and teachers have a reputation for real success in teaching English. Others have a poor reputation. For example, some people will tell you they learnt a lot of English at their school. Others will say they studied for three, four, or five years or more, and learnt almost nothing. The main test for real success in teaching and learning should be whether or not the learners can communicate at all in English. Can they understand instructions in class, or questions in an interview, or talks at a conference? Can they ask for directions in the street, or provide personal information, or explain business proposals? Can they understand simple articles, or business letters, or technical books? Can they complete application forms, or write letters or reports? Can they pass recognized examinations in English, like the UCLES exams or the TOEFL tests?

We can all recognize such real, practical success in teaching and learning English. We know success is not just being able to repeat memorized sentences or complete grammar exercises—though they may contribute to learning. Success is not the same as getting an 8, 9, or 10 in course tests—

though that may indicate some progress. It is the ability of learners to use English effectively in real communication situations.

Teachers and teaching

Successful teachers and the institutions where they teach may differ in many ways. For example, in the teachers' experience, training, and level of English, or the size of classes, hours of class per week, and the methodology and materials used. However, successful teachers tend to have certain things in common. They usually:

1 have a practical command of English, not just a knowledge of grammar rules
2 use English most of the time in every class, including beginners' classes
3 think mostly in terms of learner practice, not teacher explanations
4 find time for really communicative activities, not just practice of language forms
5 focus their teaching on learners' needs, not just on 'finishing' the syllabus or coursebook.

As far as point 1 is concerned, a teacher's development of a command of English should be a life-long hobby as well as a professional obligation. Of course, a knowledge of the rules and terminology of English grammar and vocabulary is also useful. But teaching, especially language teaching, is much more than just the transfer of knowledge. If teachers follow point 2, this means that their learners constantly experience the real communicative use of English. It increases their exposure to the language through listening comprehension, and gives them opportunities to speak English. Point 3 relates to two general observations about teaching and learning languages. First, explanations often become long, complicated discussions in the learners' native language (often referred to as their *L1*), which may leave little time for the practice and use of English. Second, most people seem to learn much more from use of a language than from explanations about it. Point 4 again recognizes that language learning is essentially about communication. And point 5 puts the learners at the centre of teaching. Your success as a teacher is based entirely on their success as learners.

Co-ordination of English language departments

Most institutions where teaching is generally successful have systems to set standards related to the five points discussed above. For example, there is careful selection of teachers. Their work is co-ordinated by means of meetings and seminars, class observation, materials, and tests. All the teachers are in general agreement about principles, goals, and methodology. There is continuity in the courses and co-operation among the teachers.

Obviously, it is better for teachers to teach and learners to study in such institutions. But even in a poorly co-ordinated institution teachers can begin to change things by teaching their own classes as effectively as they can. If they then establish some co-operation with one or two other teachers, they have started something important.

Questions

(Use your experience as a learner to answer these questions if you are not yet teaching.)

Do you agree that successful English teachers usually speak English in class?

Do you agree that they give much more time to practice than to explanation?

Do you agree that teacher co-operation in an English language department is important?

Establishing goals and objectives in teaching English

The absence of clear or appropriate goals in education is bad for both teachers and learners. At school, children and adolescents often seem to be required to study algebra, or Roman history, or English, only because these subjects are on the official curriculum and there are tests to pass. This can have a very negative effect on the learners' attitude towards these subjects. The clear definition of appropriate goals is vital to successful English language teaching and learning.

Unfortunately, not everyone recognizes real success in English language learning. Some teachers and learners do not look beyond the grammar and vocabulary currently being practised, or the next test. Also, the long-term goals of teaching are not always explicit in course syllabuses. In fact, course syllabuses, materials, and tests sometimes seem to present only a sequence of short-term objectives. Although short-term objectives are important in giving learners and teachers a feeling of making progress, it is important never to lose sight of the overall long-term goal of English language teaching, to enable learners to communicate effectively, and as far as possible accurately, in English. We will look at goals and objectives in more detail in Chapter 8.

Variations in course goals

English is taught as a foreign language in very different contexts around the world—to schoolchildren and working adults, in small and large groups, for three hours or ten hours a week. Obviously, the goals of English courses vary according to the contexts in which they are taught.

The goals of different courses may be, or at least may appear to be, any of the following:

1 to enable the learners to communicate in real English, both spoken and written
2 to enable the learners to read technical publications in real English
3 to get the learners to memorize English grammar rules and vocabulary.

We use the expression 'real English' in 1 and 2 to refer to the English used both inside and outside language classrooms: for example the English of instructions, conversations, magazines, books, airports, and the Internet. In contrast, the information about English grammar rules and vocabulary in 3 is often presented, practised, and tested in 'unreal English'. The language in the exercises and tests would seem strange to native speakers, or even confuse them. Working with 'unreal English' may give learners some useful foundations in grammar and vocabulary, but it is a long way from the use of English for real communication.

Ideally, the goal of most English language courses would be like that in 1: to develop a general command of 'real English' for use outside the classroom. If learners can communicate effectively when hearing, reading, speaking, and writing 'real English', they will manage in almost any English language situation they meet outside the classroom. But, in many contexts, factors such as the shortage of time or the large number of learners in a class make this goal seem difficult or impossible to reach. When time is short, one common response is to limit the goal to what is considered most important for the learners. For example, in 2 the goal has been intentionally limited to reading technical publications. In higher education, reading is often considered the most important skill to master.

In very difficult conditions, for example large, unmotivated groups with little time, a common response is to work towards a goal like that in 3. The goal in the official syllabus may be more like that in 1 or 2, but in practice teachers find it easier to explain English grammar and give rules and formulas for learners to memorize. However, we believe it is possible to work towards communicative goals like those in 1 or 2, even in quite difficult teaching contexts. With a group of fifteen motivated learners for five hours a week, you can easily work towards the goals in 1. With a group, or many groups, of forty initially unmotivated learners for two hours a week, goals like those in 1 will present a much greater challenge and results will inevitably be modest. But we have seen many teachers working communicatively with groups of forty or more secondary-school learners— those notorious 'difficult' adolescents—and achieving good results.

What are 'good results'? Well, when you observe a class, the first sign of good teaching is the attention and interest shown by the learners. If they are voluntarily paying attention, something good is probably happening. If they are showing clear interest—listening eagerly, following instructions, asking and answering questions, mostly in English—something very good is probably happening. Holding the learners' attention, getting their interest and their active participation, are essential in English language teaching, as in all teaching. If you do not achieve these immediate objectives in each lesson, you are unlikely to reach the long-term goals of getting learners to master the elements and systems of English and use them in communication.

Last, but not least, your teaching goals and objectives should be apparent to the learners. They should feel that every activity you do with them is worthwhile, and that the whole course is worthwhile. They should never feel that you are just filling time until the bell rings to end the class, or that you are going mechanically through the book or syllabus. Not all short-term objectives will be directly related to communicating in English. For example, you may decide that it is useful to get the learners to memorize some irregular verb forms, or find and underline all the conjunctions in a reading text. But this kind of short-term objective is really worthwhile only when it contributes towards achieving the main goal of teaching English—to develop an active repertoire of English for use outside the classroom. If you or the learners lose sight of this main goal, their motivation for learning English as a foreign language is likely to weaken.

Questions

What was the best foreign language course you have ever taken?
Why was it better than other courses (think about the teacher, the group, the book, and the activities)?
Did you feel that you were really learning to communicate in the language?

Communication first and last

If communication in English is to be perceived by the learners as the main goal of the course, English should be used for real communication in the classroom as much as possible. This means introducing some of the English needed for genuine communication early in the course, for example, that needed for routine greetings, instructions, and requests. And, depending on the overall objectives of the course, as much time as possible should also be given to realistic work on the language skills that the learners need to master, for example, conversation, reading comprehension, or written composition.

This may mean seeing your course syllabus in a new way. It may seem on the surface that the most important element in the syllabus is a sequence of new language items. However, if you look more carefully, you will probably find that you are also expected to enable the learners to communicate in real situations. You may also find that you are expected to run the class mostly in English, avoiding complicated discussion of the new language items in the learners' native language.

To do this successfully, especially with beginners, you will need techniques that allow you to focus on new language items without using the learners' first language much. We will be looking at some of these in Chapters 2, 3, and 4. You will also need techniques for establishing and developing English as the main classroom language, for if you simply 'speak English all the time' you will quickly drive beginners, and even more advanced learners, to despair!

English as the main classroom language

Among the many possible uses of English in the classroom are:

- greetings and farewells, for example: 'Good morning. How are you?'; 'See you tomorrow.'
- instructions, for example: 'Open your books at page sixty-two. Look at the picture.'
- enquiries, for example: 'Can you see, David? Would you like to move over here?'
- feedback, for example: 'That's interesting, Maria. Very good.'
- chat, for example, calling roll: 'Tony . . . No? Where is he today? Does anyone know?'

Many of these interactions recur naturally, class after class. They can quickly become routines for the learners, just as they would learn common interactions if they were living in an English-speaking country. Some teachers try to introduce English in the classroom little by little, using the learners' first language most of the time at first. This is rather like trying to give up smoking little by little—it hardly ever works. One of your first objectives in an English language course, even with beginners, should be to establish English as the main classroom language.

Teaching ideas

Here are some of the most useful techniques for presenting new English expressions for use in the classroom:

- **Demonstration with actions and objects**
  For example, close your own book as you say 'Close your books', hold up a sheet of paper as you say 'Take a sheet of paper, one sheet of paper', or draw columns on the board as you say 'Draw three columns like this'.

- **Gesture and mime**
  For example, make the typical gesture with your hand as you say 'Stand up', 'Come here', or 'Sit down'; mime writing as you say 'Write the answers', or mime distributing things as you say 'Please give out these photocopies'.

- **Paraphrase**
  Use a *cognate* expression, that is, one similar to an expression in the learners' first language—for example, 'That's correct' helps Spanish learners understand 'That's right', and 'Excellent' helps them understand 'Very good'.

- **Translation into English**
  For example, learners may say in their L1 'What does that mean?', 'I don't understand', or 'Will you repeat that?' You can put the English versions of such useful expressions on cards on the wall and point to them when necessary. Add cards for new expressions as you introduce them.

- **Translation**
  Give the translation of the new expression the first time you use it, but after that get a learner to demonstrate or, if necessary, translate.

Constant, consistent use of routine classroom expressions in English soon gets learners accustomed to them. Once your learners are familiar with an expression, stop supporting it with demonstration, gesture, mime, paraphrase, or translation. However, remember that if classroom language becomes too varied too soon, it can overwhelm some learners and demotivate them. To start with, control the range of language you use: speak naturally, but fairly slowly and carefully. You would probably do the same outside the classroom with non-native speakers of your language. Increase the range and speed of classroom English gradually as learners advance.

Of course, with groups that share a first language, occasional use of it is appropriate, for example:

- to discuss briefly feelings about the course, progress, and plans
- to clarify ideas or instructions that are more complex than usual
- to make a useful comparison between English and the first language.

And you can never entirely stop the learners comparing English with their first language and translating in their own heads. This is both natural and beyond your control.

In some cases it may seem impossible to cover the syllabus using English most of the time. But the important question is whether 'covering the syllabus' using the learners' first language most of the time really produces worthwhile learning. At the end of the course, can they actually *do* anything with English—understand it or express themselves in it effectively to some degree? If they cannot, you may have nothing to lose and a lot to gain by switching from their first language to English as the main classroom language. You can often motivate learners towards this switch by discussing it briefly with them—in their first language, of course.

Of course, using English as the main classroom language can be a learning opportunity and a challenge for non-native teachers of English as well as for learners. The teachers practise their own English more, but may also make a few mistakes. For example, speakers of many languages often say *'Very well' instead of 'Very good', and *'I want that you work in pairs' instead of 'I want you to work in pairs'. Many teachers may need to do a little research into classroom English (we have listed some useful books in the Sources and Further Reading section at the end of this book). But a few mistakes are far outweighed by the benefits of using English in the classroom: it can get learners to feel that they are really using English for a purpose.

Routine communicative activities

If you take all the natural opportunities to use English for communication in the classroom, you remind the learners of the main goal of the course. If you create additional opportunities, you send an even stronger message. If you do not take and make such opportunities, you send them the message that the purpose of the course is just to learn information about the language and pass tests. This means that many learners are likely to lose motivation and see English as just another compulsory subject in the academic curriculum.

One regular opportunity for an extra communicative activity is the 'warm-up' at the beginning of each lesson. Some teachers begin most lessons with a review of the language items practised in the previous lesson. This approach—almost always starting lessons with a focus on language—tends to make learners see the learning of language forms, structures, and rules as the main purpose of the course. The teaching seems to be directed towards short-term objectives only—learning one item after another for the next test. Instead, you can start lessons with real communication in English. Without focusing obviously on any specific language forms, engage the learners in a simple communicative activity, using language they already know. Here are some examples of communicative warm-ups. They are all suitable for elementary-level classes, but the last ones require more English than the first ones. They should each take from five to ten minutes.

Teaching ideas

- Go through a flexible conversational routine with the group, for example:

Teacher	Good morning. How are you today?
Learners	Fine, thank you. And you?
Teacher	So-so. You're happy this morning, Ana.
Learner 1	Yes . . . er . . . my birthday.
Teacher	Ah, it's your birthday! How old are you?
Learner 1	Fourteen.
Teacher	Congratulations! Is there another birthday this week? No? Just Ana? Well . . . what's the date today?
Learner 2	It's Thursday, March 14th.
Teacher	Right. Who can write that on the board?

- Tell the group about a pet—for example, the kind of animal, its name, size, colour, age, and what it eats. Then say you—or a relative—have another pet, and invite the learners to ask questions, for example, 'What kind of animal is it?'; 'What is its name?' Then write the start of a conversation on the board:

  A Have you got a pet?
  B Yes, I have./No, I haven't.
  A Has one of your relatives got one?
  B Yes, my _____ has one.

  Get the learners to talk about pets in pairs using the conversation on the board as a guide. Afterwards, ask about the most unusual pets.

  The same basic idea can be used with other topics, for example, a neighbour, or a relative living in another city—but asking about where they work or study, not what they eat! It can even be used about a bicycle or car.

- Ask one or two learners about something they did last weekend using question-words like 'what', 'where', 'who with', and 'why'. Then get learners to ask you about something you did last weekend. Finally, get the learners to talk in pairs, starting: 'What was the most interesting thing you did last weekend?' The same idea can be used about other topics such as 'on your last holiday' and 'last year'—or plans for next weekend.

- Distribute pictures cut out from recent magazines to pairs of learners. Get pairs to discuss questions such as who the people are, where they are, what they are doing, why they are in the news, and anything else the learners know about them.

A third way of emphasizing the communicative goal of a course is to include at least one communicative skills activity (see Chapters 5 and 6) in every lesson. This may require a special effort on your part. The presentation, practice, and review of language items take up a lot of time in many courses, and your syllabus, course materials, and tests may make little or no provision for skills work. In that case, you will have to find activities yourself. It is important to respond to this challenge if your teaching is to be really effective.

A general model of English teaching

Throughout this chapter so far, we have been emphasizing communication as the starting point of an English language course as well as the main goal of teaching English. This makes English language teaching look like a simple 'communication highway':

TEFL =
C O M M U N I C A T I O N ⟶ GOAL

But we have also recognized that a sequence of new language items is usually a major element in course syllabuses. Each item is to be presented, practised, and somehow incorporated into a growing repertoire of English. This cycle is often described as 'Presentation-Practice-Production' (usually shortened to PPP). This is a useful and widely-recognized model of language teaching. It can be added to the 'communication highway' view of English language teaching as a series of 'PPP loops':

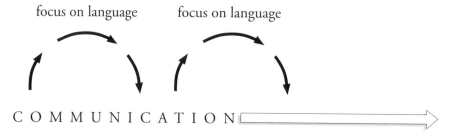

focus on language   focus on language

C O M M U N I C A T I O N ⟶

We also said that learning how to communicate effectively and accurately in English is a long-term project, and that even basic errors persist in learners' conversation and writing for a long time. Learners do not often grasp new items perfectly and permanently at first. They usually need a lot of further work, often long after first presentation and practice. We can add this to the 'communication highway' too:

C O M M U N I C A T I O N

later focus on language   later focus on language

With communication as the beginning and end of teaching and learning English, but 'presentation and practice of new language loops' and 'language review and-error-correction loops' as important elements, we have a complete model of English teaching which can help us see the complex process of teaching more clearly.

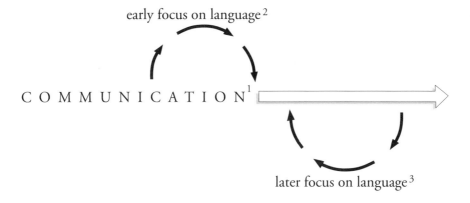

early focus on language[2]

C O M M U N I C A T I O N[1]

later focus on language[3]

Our discussion of the methodology of teaching English has already begun in this chapter. We have said that it is important to begin by establishing English as the main classroom language, and to take and make every opportunity to involve the learners in its use for communication (1 in the model). In Chapters 2, 3, and 4 we shall be looking at ways of working on new language items in the syllabus (2 in the model). Then in Chapters 5 and 6 with developing communicative skills (continuing 1 in the model, but also contributing to 3). In Chapter 7 we look at previously encountered language (3 in the model).

Of course, although a clear model or approach to teaching is very useful, it is a simplification and an idealization. Reality is more complex, and any model needs adapting to specific teaching situations. Also, certain conditions are necessary for any approach to teaching to work adequately in practice.

Creating conditions for learning

Certain classroom conditions help a lot in the teaching of any subject: for example, sufficient space, a group that is not too big, adequate lighting, and a room with good acoustics that is neither too hot nor too cold. But good material conditions do not ensure successful learning, and poor material conditions do not necessarily prevent it. More important for successful language teaching and learning are other, less tangible, conditions, for example, plenty of opportunities for learners to participate in class and an atmosphere in which they feel motivated to learn. Teachers can often do more about the intangible conditions than the material ones.

Learner participation

Groups of learners vary greatly. Some are all you could wish for, but others are hard to control or direct, or passive and difficult to inspire. Getting and keeping your learners' attention and their positive participation may be one of your greatest challenges. And it is not always the most energetic teachers that create the most dynamic lessons. They may do a lot themselves, but get the learners to do very little. Even during an 'explanation' phase in a lesson, you can involve the learners actively rather than making them listen passively. Here is an example of *elicitation*, in other words, asking the learners questions so that they actively discover English grammar rather than just being told about it:

Teacher	[*pointing to a group of adjectives on the board*] Which of these adjectives use 'more'?
Learner 1	'Expensive', 'comfortable', 'modern' . . .
Learner 2	. . . 'attractive'.
Teacher	Right—'expensive', 'comfortable', 'modern', and 'attractive'. And which use '-er'?
Learner 3	'Big', 'cheap' . . .
Learner 4	. . . 'old' . . .
Learner 5	. . . 'small'.
Teacher	Right. How are these two types of adjective different?
Learner 2	'Big', 'cheap', 'old', 'small', are . . . um . . . small, one-syll—um . . .
Teacher	Exactly—one-syllable adjectives. And they form the comparative with . . . ?
Learner 6	'-er'—'bigger', 'cheaper' . . .
Teacher	That's right. And 'more' is used with . . .
Learner 1	Long adjectives—'more expensive', 'more comfortable' . . .
Teacher	Right. Let's put that on the board in two columns—adjective plus '-er' on the left, and 'more' plus adjective on the right.

In the above example, the interaction pattern is 'teacher → learner/s'. This is the commonest pattern of interaction in most classrooms. Often it takes the form of 'teacher explanation → learner silence' or 'teacher model → learner choral repetition'. But these involve the learners much less than the 'teacher question → learner response' pattern above. However, offering opportunities for learners to participate actively in lessons does not always get a positive response. Some teachers despair, saying 'I've asked questions, I've set tasks, I've put the learners in pairs and groups—I've tried everything—but they just sit there and say and do nothing.' If learners are to participate willingly in class they must understand what is expected of them. Questions, activities, and pair or groupwork should be carefully planned to enable learners to participate. You should ask yourself questions like 'Do the learners know the English needed for the activity?' and 'Have I explained clearly what they have to do?'

Even when the learners know the necessary English and what to do in an activity, they will not participate if they lack confidence. They must not be afraid to speak up in front of you and other learners. It takes time to build up confidence, and it comes initially from your example and leadership. You set the tone for all classroom behaviour through your own reactions to learner participation, the way you encourage the learners and deal with problems. Most learners will not want to participate if you say 'No! Wrong!' every time they make a mistake, or 'Come on! Come on!' every time they hesitate. And weaker learners will not risk humiliation if you turn in exasperation to a better learner every time they falter.

When you start teaching a new group, you need to spend some time on helping them get used to your way of doing things. It is best, first of all, to use simple activities and then move on to more complex ones. Frequent activities in pairs and groups are good for building confidence. Especially for shy learners, they offer a less threatening environment than whole-class work.

Motivation

Most teachers consider motivation essential for successful language learning. However, motivation is difficult to define and measure. Are all learners motivated by worthwhile goals and clear objectives, the constant use of English in the classroom, a variety of activities and interactions, and sensitive handling of errors and hesitations? Our assumption has been that they are. But we recognize that motivation is a complex phenomenon, and not all learners respond to teaching in the same way.

Certain aspects of motivation may be beyond your influence. Some learners come to a course needing English immediately for study or work, or wanting to learn it because they love 'Anglo–American culture'. Others may be more reluctant, but know they are likely to need English in the future. Yet others are obliged to take a course, but have no desire to learn English, and a sincere hope they will never need to use it. With the first type of learner, the challenge is to maintain and exploit the motivation they bring to the course. With the last type, the challenge is to work hard at making the course itself enjoyable and satisfying. You also have to try to get reluctant learners to recognize that, for virtually anyone, English really could be useful at some time in their lives.

Even for initially reluctant learners, appropriate goals and objectives can give direction and the will to work—in other words, improve motivation. And any success in real communication can motivate. But 'an ability to communicate effectively in English' is such a huge, ill-defined goal, quite remote for most elementary learners. Worthwhile and achievable short-term objectives can give the learners satisfaction and a sense of success as they work towards the main goal of their course.

Even the most carefully planned activities will normally motivate learners only if they are related to their interests, needs, and aspirations. You should try to find out what these are and plan lessons accordingly. For example, teenage learners may want some work on communicating in English via the Internet, or activities using popular songs. It is a good idea to consult with your learners about topics and activities, and get them to bring to class materials they are interested in.

Topics can be a rich source of motivation in the English language classroom. There are topics of personal interest, for example, music, films, cars, computers, the Internet, pets, and sports. If your learners are interested in Britain, the USA, or another English-speaking country, a coursebook with that country as the main theme can provide a good supply of topics. You may also be able to use authentic materials from those countries, for example, magazine and newspaper articles, cassettes of songs, and videos of television programmes.

Of course, English does not 'belong' to any specific countries, societies, or cultures. These days, there are more non-native than native speakers of English and it is more often used between two non-native speakers than between a non-native and a native speaker. This cosmopolitan perspective, common in several more recent coursebooks, appeals to many learners and is a rich source of topics for activities and lesson themes. Again, you may be able to use authentic materials, including any English-language newspapers published in your own country.

Personalities and relationships are important for motivation. Your personality is bound to appeal to some learners more than others. You cannot totally change yourself, but you can modify or develop some things.

For example, you can use the learners' names and show a personal interest in them, and take care to behave in a fair way towards all learners alike. You can also educate yourself in topics that interest your learners, for example, pop music and films for teenagers, new cars and technical developments for mechanics.

Although, ideally, learners should be motivated by an awareness of their own progress, many will rely mostly on your feedback. It can be very motivating for them if you tell them clearly that you are pleased with their effort and progress. It may even be a wonderful surprise after frequent expressions of dissatisfaction from previous teachers!

Summary

In Chapter 1 we have considered the following points:

Recognizing success in teaching English. Real success in English language teaching and learning is when the learners can actually communicate in English inside and outside the classroom. Successful teachers and institutions differ in many ways, but tend to have certain things in common. Among these are routine communication in English in class, an emphasis on practice rather than explanation, and co-operation among teachers.

Establishing goals and objectives in teaching English. A major goal of all English language teaching should be to enable learners to use English effectively, and as far as possible accurately, in communication. Memorizing language forms and rules is valid as a short-term objective, but not as a main goal. Where time is short and groups large, goals may be limited, for example, to reading technical publications, but they should still involve communication. Some immediate objectives will not be communicative in themselves, but should clearly contribute to the development of communicative ability. Learners should feel there is a worthwhile purpose to each activity and the whole course. Among the most important objectives of every lesson is engaging the learners' attention and interest.

Communication first and last. The communicative goal of a course should be ever-present. It should be emphasized from the start by establishing English as the main classroom language. This requires careful management and the use of specific techniques. Regular communicative activities, such as warm-ups, also emphasize the communicative nature and goal of a course. Communicating in English and learning the English language go hand in hand.

A general model of English teaching. Communication should be the main goal of all English teaching, but the presentation and practice of new language items is a major element in most syllabuses. We must also recognize that learning language items and systems and eliminating errors is a long-term project. These three elements—communication, new language, and continuing work on old language—can be integrated into a general model with a 'communication highway' and presentation-practice and review-remedial loops. A model can help us see a complex process more clearly, but it is a simplification and idealization. It must be adapted to specific situations.

Creating conditions for learning. Material conditions are not as important for successful learning as other, less tangible, conditions such as opportunities for learners to participate in class, and an atmosphere in which they feel motivated to learn. Lessons should be dynamic, involving the learners in varied activities and interactions. Learners should be active, not just listen and repeat. To participate willingly, they must feel able and confident, not threatened by failure, reprimand, or ridicule. You must take the lead in establishing a positive atmosphere, planning appropriate activities, encouraging learners and dealing with problems sensitively. Motivation is essential for learning. Some types of motivation are brought or not brought to the course by learners, for example, a real need for English. Others can be promoted or created by you—for example, enjoyment of topics, activities, and interactions. Your relationship and rapport with the group and individual learners is also very important.

Project

Focusing on classroom English

Purpose: To specify the repertoire of English for an elementary classroom.
Procedure:
1 Select and study part of a lesson from an elementary coursebook.
2 List the English expressions you think you would need to teach the lesson. You can write out a probable script for the lesson if you wish.
3 Where you are in doubt, check the grammar, vocabulary, and pronunciation of the expressions (in a grammar book or dictionary, or with a native-speaker).
4 Consider how you would present the meaning of some of these expressions to the learners if you were introducing them for the first time.
5 If you are actually going to teach the lesson, note how the learners respond to your greetings, instructions, and comments. You could even record part of the lesson on an audio-cassette and listen to it at home.

2 PRESENTING NEW LANGUAGE ITEMS

Introduction

In this chapter we look at the ways in which new language items are presented in syllabuses and coursebooks. When learners encounter new items they need to know what they mean and how they are used in communication. They also usually need to know how to pronounce them, their grammatical structure, and how they relate to other language items. All these aspects of new items are usually dealt with best by introducing them in a context in which they are normally used. It is generally convenient to present the spoken form before the written form. Presentation usually leads immediately into practice of the new item.

New items in an English language course

New language items will probably be prominent, even dominant, in your syllabus or coursebook, and of course learners must learn new grammar and vocabulary in order to make progress in English. However, it is important to remember that learners need to be able to do more than just remember and repeat new items; they must be able to use them actively to communicate.

Most of the new items you are expected to teach will normally be indicated in your syllabus or coursebook. Here, for example, is part of the contents page of a typical book:

Not all coursebooks or syllabuses indicate the items to be taught in the same way, but this kind of division is typical of most modern materials. *Functions* are the communicative things we do with language. New functional items may be indicated only with a description of the function, for example:

BOOK 2   CONTENTS

Unit	Topics	Functions	Language
1	Famous cities	Describing/comparing places Making reservations	Comparison with adjectives *I'd like to . . .* *Wh*-questions
2	Personal plans Arrangements	Making arrangements Making excuses	Present Progressive for Future *Let's . . .* *I'm afraid . . .*

Introducing yourself
Expressing likes and dislikes

or models of language commonly used to carry out the functions may also be given, for example:

Introductions: *Hello. I'm Michael.*
Likes/dislikes: *I like cats. I don't like dogs. Mary likes dogs. She doesn't like cats.*

New grammatical items may be indicated with grammatical terminology, for example:

Present Continuous
Comparisons with adjectives

or models of the structures may be given:

What's Mary doing? She's swimming.
Glasgow is bigger than Edinburgh. Edinburgh is more famous than Glasgow.

No matter how new items are indicated, you will almost certainly be dealing with new functions and new grammar. Both types of item, and new vocabulary, are usually connected in a unit or lesson. For example, a lesson may deal with the function 'Talking about routine activities'. This will probably mean teaching the grammatical structure 'The Simple Present Tense' and vocabulary such as 'get up', 'take a shower', 'have breakfast' and 'go to school'.

Questions

Examine your syllabus or coursebook (or, if you are not teaching at present, one you might use) and see how new items are indicated. Do you feel clear about what you would have to teach? How would you clarify any doubts?

What you need to know about new items

There are several aspects of new items that you may need to know about and learners may need to learn. First, it is always necessary to know the meaning of new items; for example, 'good night' is equivalent to 'goodbye' in the evening or at night. It is also necessary to know about their use in communication; for example, in some languages the same form is used to say 'hello' and 'goodbye' at night, but 'good night' is used exclusively to say 'goodbye', never 'hello'. In other words, it is a farewell, never a greeting.

It is usually necessary to know how new forms are pronounced and written. For example, in spite of its spelling, 'good night' is pronounced /gʊd naɪt/, not /goːd nɪgt/. It is usually useful to understand how *compound* forms (i.e. forms which contain more than one word) are structured. For example, 'good night' is structured the same as 'good morning' (adjective + noun). It may be useful to know how one form relates to another. For example, the 'good morning/afternoon/evening/night' relationship. It may also be necessary to know about other aspects of grammar. For example, adjectives in English normally precede the noun and have no plural form, so it is 'good books' (not *'books good' or *'goods books').

It is also worth considering what is really new for your learners. In a beginners' course for young learners at primary or secondary level, you can assume that virtually all the 'new' items in the course will indeed be new for all the learners. However, if you are teaching older 'false beginners' (learners who are repeating the beginning stages) or intermediate learners of any age, it is probable that some will know or partially know virtually every 'new' item in the course.

In the first case—with young beginners—you will probably have to give examples of each item. In the second case, you can interest and motivate the learners more if you *elicit*—that is, get examples of items from one or more learners and then use them to teach the item to those learners who do not know or remember it.

Question

Can you anticipate any difficulties your learners might have with the following items because of their native language?

Good afternoon/evening/night
/gʊd ɑːftənuːn/ iːvnɪŋ/ naɪt/

I've got a stomach ache/ cold/ temperature
/aɪv gɒt ə stʌmək eɪk/ kəʊld/ temprɪtʃə/

Functional-grammatical items

We have said that the major new language items specified in most syllabuses or coursebooks are functions or grammatical structures. We are going to deal with them together because there is usually a very close relationship between them. In your syllabus or in the table of contents of your coursebook you probably have one column headed 'Functions' and another headed 'Language', 'Grammar', or 'Structures'. Not long ago, there would not have been a 'Functions' column. Teachers thought only in terms of 'teaching the language'—the grammar and vocabulary. Then linguists and language teachers began to emphasize that language is a communication system used for practical purposes. These purposes are the 'functions' or 'communicative functions' listed in most syllabuses and coursebook tables of contents. One aspect of what are called 'functions' in syllabuses and coursebooks is what we do with language in communicative interactions, for example, to greet people, to introduce ourselves, and to apologize. Another aspect of these 'functions' is the expression of notions such as name and address, time (for example, future events), and place (for example, asking for and giving directions).

The important point to remember is that language teaching is now usually approached from a communicative angle, emphasizing what learners may need to actually do and say with English. Of course, learners still need grammar and vocabulary to do and say communicative things, to communicate. But the language in most courses today is selected and organized in response to these practical communicative functions rather than with the idea of presenting 'all the grammar' of the language.

The language for some functions consists essentially of vocabulary items—words or expressions, for example:

Greeting people: *Hello. Good morning.*
Suggesting courses of action: *Let's . . . Why not . . . ?*

However, the language for most functions consists of a grammatical structure, or a set of structures, that is, a grammatical system, for example:

Stating/asking about occupations:

What	do	you		do?
	does	your	mother	
			father	

I		am		
My	mother	is	a	student.
	father			teacher.
				doctor.

Some syllabuses and coursebooks emphasize the communicative aspect, for example:

Persuading:

I recommend Acapulco. It's cheaper than Cancún. There are lots of good hotels. And the weather's more stable than in Cancún.

Other syllabuses and coursebooks emphasize the notional aspect, for example:

Making comparisons:

Acapulco is older than Cancún. Cancún is smaller than Acapulco. Cancún is more expensive than Acapulco. Acapulco is more spectacular than Cancún.

You need to be aware of both the communicative and the notional aspects of what syllabuses and coursebooks call 'functions', and decide how to deal with them best in your own teaching situation.

Presenting new functional-grammatical items

Apart from the considerations we have looked at above, you should plan how to involve the learners actively in the presentation and practice of new functional-grammatical items.

Teaching analysis and planning

In order to teach a functional-grammatical item effectively, you must first understand that item yourself. You should know its meaning, how it is used in communication, how it is structured, its pronunciation and spelling, and the grammatical relationships and rules which affect it. You should also be able to anticipate the specific problems your learners are likely to have with it.

Much of this information may be carefully considered in your coursebook, but international courses cannot take account of every problem for specific language groups, for example, the tendency of Spanish-speaking learners to soften or drop final consonants and to omit pronoun subjects, or the difficulty Russian-speaking learners have with reading and writing Roman script or using 'am', 'is', and 'are'. Only you, the teacher, can do that.

Here are some notes made by a Mexican secondary-school teacher about to teach 'stating/asking about occupations':

OCCUPATIONS

Structures/models:

What does s/he do?
S/He's a/an singer/actor/actress/film director/composer.

What do you do?
I'm a/an _____ .

1 Treat questions as formulas 'asking about occupation', not Present Simple structures (but highlight 'does s/he—do you' change).

2 Highlight 'a/an'.

3 Normal stress on final 'do' and on occupation. Weak form for auxiliary 'do/does':

   What d's she DO? She's a SINGer.

4 Highlight first/penultimate syllable stress in vocabulary:

   SINGer/ACTor/ACTress/diRECTor/comPOser.

Context:

Famous people at an international film festival reception— Sting/Enya/Nicole Kidman/Tom Cruise/Isabel Allende/Stephen Spielberg/Bebu Silvetti/Denis Rodman—and role-play for 'you/I'

Materials:

Magazine cut-out collage of a television screen showing people at the reception, plus recorded songs/film music, plus role cards.

This teacher has decided not to use the material in her coursebook (it consists of pictures of, for example, a policeman and a nurse, with 'Bob is a policeman' and 'Mary is a nurse', printed under them, and a question-answer exercise: 'In pairs, ask and answer questions like: What does Bob do? He is a policeman.'). Instead, she plans to use a situation that she hopes will engage her learners' interest more and make the presentation and initial practice more realistic. She will extend the vocabulary later, including the occupations in the book and others relevant to her learners, for example, their parents' occupations, and what they themselves want to be.

In her notes, she is taking into consideration the following points:

- *Meaning/concept.* She plans to present models related to a clearly defined group of occupations—those related to the film industry. This will be in the context of an international film festival reception on television. She will use a collage 'television screen' of magazine cut-outs of the people and film advertisements, plus excerpts from songs and film music.

- *Use in communication.* She plans to organize 'conversation' about the people:

  A Look, that's Denis Rodman!
  B What does he do?
  A He's a basketball player and an actor.
  B Oh yes, of course.

  She will also use a role-play, with each learner as a famous person at the crowded reception:

  A Hi. What do you do?
  B I'm a composer.
  A Oh, you're Bebu Silvetti!
  B That's right. What do you do?
  A I'm _____ .

- *Structure.* She intends to highlight—that is, draw attention to—the use of 'a/an' with occupations. No article is used in Spanish and her learners will be tempted to say *'He's singer.' Although she plans to treat the questions as formulas rather than as examples of the Present Simple, she still intends to make the 'does s/he ↔ do you' change clear.

- *Pronunciation.* She plans to deal with specific problems her learners might have. She plans to indicate weak forms and last-word sentence stress:

  What d'y' DO? I'ma SINger.
  What d's s'e DO? He'sa comPOser.

  She also plans to make a general point about word stress. English usually has penultimate syllable stress in words ending -or/-ress/-er, while Spanish has final syllable stress with the corresponding words ending -or/riz, for example:

  English: ACtor, ACtress, diRECtor
  Spanish: acTOR, actRIZ, direcTOR

  The written form is not considered in her notes as she plans to teach it in a future lesson.

– *Grammar.* She does not plan to explain the auxiliaries 'do/does'. Teachers often find themselves explaining that in this context these words indicate a question and do not have a dictionary meaning, unlike the main verb 'do' ('work at'). This teacher would apparently prefer to avoid such an 'explanation' or 'discussion' if possible, since it can make an essentially simple formula seem mysteriously illogical and complicated for many learners.

There are probably many other practical details in her head, but in these notes she has covered the most important points for presentation, and the beginning of practice. Even if she had decided to use the textbook material, she would still have needed to do some of the same analysis and planning to convert the material into a clear, interesting lesson.

Presentation procedures

In your plan, you need to consider the specific procedures you will use in the classroom. Here, we will look at the presentation stage and the beginning of practice only. In the lesson extracts below, the Present Progressive is being presented to a secondary-school class. This teacher has chosen a situation that he hopes will appeal to his 11 and 12 year-old learners, that of astronauts on a space shuttle.

Extract 1

Teacher	Look at this picture. Do you know what it is?
Learner 1	Discovery.
Teacher	Right, Maria! It's the space shuttle 'Discovery'. What do you know about it?
Learner 2	It's American.

Learner 3	Yes, but . . . Spanish astronauta . . . Pedro Duque.
Teacher	Yes, Spanish, Japanese, Russian astronauts go in it with Americans. Very good, David. So this is a space shuttle and this is a rocket. Listen—rocket, rocket. Everyone.
Learners	Rocket.
Teacher	Good. Listen—space shuttle, space shuttle.
Learners	Space shuttle.
Teacher	Again.
Learners	Space shuttle.
Teacher	Good. Now, are all these people astronauts?
Learner 4	No, astronauts and tecni . . . tecni . . .
Teacher	Right, Eric. These are technicians. What else is there in the picture? Other things?
Learner 5	There are photographs.
Teacher	Right, Susana, phoTOgraphers. A PHOtograph is a picture, a PHOto. These people are phoTOgraphers. Are the astronauts in the space shuttle?
Learner 6	No. They're out.
Teacher	Right, they're outside the shuttle. Does anyone want to be an astronaut? What are your ambitions—astronaut, space technician, doctor, engineer?
Learner 7	Astronaut, teacher.
Teacher	You want to be an astronaut?
Learner 8	Yes.
Teacher	And you, Maria?

Extract 2

Teacher	Now, look at this picture. The rocket and shuttle are going up. They're going up into space. Now the shuttle's separating from the rocket. Now look—this is the earth. And here's the shuttle. The shuttle's orbiting the earth. The shuttle—IS—orbitING—the earth. Orbit-ING . . . orbiting. The shuttle—IS . . . The shuttle'S . . . The shuttle's—orbiting the earth. Listen—The SHUTtle's ORBiting the EARTH. The SHUTtle's ORBiting the EARTH. Everyone.
Learners	The shuttle's orbiting the earth.
Teacher	Again.
Learners	The shuttle's orbiting the earth.
Teacher	Good. Lorena.
Learner 1	The shuttle's orbiting the earth.
Teacher	Good. Mario.
Learner 2	The shuttle's orbiting the earth.
Teacher	Good. Let's look at the sequence again. Here the rocket and shuttle are going up into space. And here the shuttle's . . . mm?
Learner 3	Separating from the rocket.
Teacher	Very good! The shuttle's separating from the rocket. And here . . .
Learner	The shuttle's orbiting the earth.
Teacher	Right! So what about this picture, Ingrid?
Learner 4	The rocket and shuttle is . . . are going up into space.
T	And this picture, Susana?

Extract 3

Teacher	Now let's look inside the shuttle. Here we are. This is Vicky Rivas, the captain. This is Rocky Moro, the pilot. This is Marc Duchamp, a biologist. And this is Yuri Rostov, an engineer. Who's this, Ana?
Learner 1	Yuri Rostov, an engineer.
Teacher	Good. And this, Eric?
Learner 2	Vicky Rivas, the captain.
Teacher	Good. Now, what are they doing? Look at Vicky. Anyone?
Learner 3	Write . . . She write.
Teacher	Yes, she's writing a report. What's she doing? Ana?
Learner 3	She's write . . . writing a report.
Teacher	Good! Can you repeat that, Marco?
Learner 4	She's writing a report.
Teacher	Yes. She's writing a report. Everyone.
Learners	She's writing a report.
Teacher	Good . . . she's writing a report in the space shuttle. And what is the space shuttle doing?
Learner 4	It's orbiting the earth.
Teacher	OK! So, Vicky's writing a report. What about the others? Rocky? Mm, what's this? A hamburger? What's Rocky doing? Anyone?
Learner 5	Rocky is eat a hamburger.
Teacher	Pardon, Eric? Eat?
Learner 5	Er . . . Rocky's eating a hamburger.
Teacher	Very good! What about Marc? Ah, this is a coffee, right. What's Marc doing? Anyone?
Learner 6	Marc's drinking a coffee.
Teacher	That's right! And Yuri?
Learner 7	Yuri's sleeping.
Teacher	Right! Now listen carefully—Yuri sleeps a lot, and at the moment he's . . .
Learners	. . . sleeping.
Teacher	Rocky eats a lot, and at . . .
Learners	. . . the moment he's eating a hamburger.
Teacher	Vicky works a lot, and . . .
Learners	. . . and at this moment she's writing a report.

If we analyse the three lesson extracts we can see a number of clear stages and techniques. The teacher does not use a rigid method, but he is quite methodical. In each extract he has one major purpose, and he uses specific techniques to achieve his objectives.

In Extract 1, the context or situation for the presentation of the Present Progressive is established. The teacher tries to involve the learners, and manages at times to make this stage fairly conversational, for example, when he asks about 'Discovery' and the learners' own ambitions. Of course, this conversational element is restricted by the fairly low level and the compulsory nature of this English class. At higher levels and with naturally motivated learners, the conversational element can be developed more.

In Extract 2, the first models of the Present Progressive are presented. The meaning is clear from the pictures, and the teacher probably also uses gestures, for example, indicating 'going up', 'separating', and 'orbiting' with his hands. The grammar is made clear by highlighting the key elements:

> **Teacher**   The shuttle—IS—orbitING—the earth. Orbit-ING . . . orbiting. The shuttle IS—The shuttle'S . . . The shuttle's—orbiting the earth.

The pronunciation is taught through getting the learners to listen to fairly naturally spoken models, and then imitate them, chorally and individually:

> **Teacher**   Listen—The SHUTtle's ORBiting the EARTH. The SHUTtle's ORBiting the EARTH. Everyone.
> **Learners**   The shuttle's orbiting the earth.

In Extract 3, the learners' understanding of the form and its use is checked. The teacher elicits more examples from the learners, using verbs they have already seen with the Present Simple, to check that they have grasped the 'IS verbING' pattern:

> **Teacher**   . . . Mm, what's this? A hamburger? What's Rocky doing? Anyone?
> **Learner 5**   Rocky is eat a hamburger.
> **Teacher**   Pardon, Eric? Eat?
> **Learner 5**   Er . . . Rocky's eating a hamburger.
> **Teacher**   Very good!

Then the teacher checks the learners' grasp of the distinction between the use of the Present Simple and the Present Progressive, emphasizing 'at the moment':

> **Teacher**   Now listen carefully—Yuri sleeps a lot, and at the moment he's . . .
> **Learners**   . . . sleeping.
> **Teacher**   Rocky eats a lot, and at . . .
> **Learners**   . . . the moment he's eating a hamburger.
> **Teacher**   Vicky works a lot, and . . .
> **Learners**   . . . at the moment she's writing a report.

This general procedure is represented diagrammatically in Figure 2.1.

Establish a context → (Extract 1)	Present key model/s → (Extract 2)	Check understanding (Extract 3)
Involve the learners in building up a context or situation which makes the meaning and use of the new item as clear as possible, and which also engages the learners' interest and imagination as much as possible.	Give (or elicit from the learners) a clear model of the new item. Make the grammar clear by highlighting the key elements. Get the learners to listen and imitate the normal pronunciation of the model.	Check the learners' grasp of the grammar by eliciting more examples of the new item. Through this elicitation in context, check understanding of meaning and use.

Figure 2.1: Stages in presenting a new language item

It is very important to remember that learners do not learn from presentation alone, or even presentation followed by practice. This first focus on new language items is only a beginning, and the learners must continually use the language for communication. You will probably have to focus on most basic functional-grammatical items again from time to time, right through to intermediate level and beyond.

The sequence of steps described above usually provides an effective way of presenting new functional-grammatical items, but it should not be seen as a rigid, mechanical procedure. You are not only teaching English, but also learners, and you need to respond to their human behaviour, often rather unpredictable. You may find, for example, that the learners do not know some of the vocabulary items that you expected them to understand, or that they easily master some aspect of pronunciation with which you expected problems.

Different functional-grammatical items in English also require some flexibility. Some items, for example, are more typical in the written language than in the spoken language. The oral presentation steps given above may then be preceded or substituted by written examples. Other items are grammatically very simple but their meaning and use is complex or subtle, in which case there may be much more emphasis on the context and concept from the beginning and less attention to the structure, for example, 'should', contrasted with 'must' and 'have to'.

Coursebook material

We have considered how teachers can prepare for and carry out the presentation and early practice of new items with their own ideas and materials. It is good to do this as much as you can since no coursebook writer knows your learners' specific needs and interests, and your own teaching style, as well as you do. But, especially at the beginning of your teaching career, you will probably need to use a lot of the presentation and practice material in your coursebook. Even experienced teachers do not usually have time to prepare everything themselves, and both institutions and learners often demand regular use of the coursebook. We will look at the use of coursebooks in more detail in Chapter 7.

The place of writing in presentation

In the procedure suggested above, the written form would usually be introduced after oral presentation, and probably oral practice. It is usually better to present items orally first and the written form later on, especially at beginner and elementary levels. There are at least two advantages to this. First, it is easier to get the learners' attention and interest with a context or situation created orally than with a text printed in a book or sentences written on the board. Second, written forms in English can exert a strong distorting influence on learners' pronunciation, for example, if Spanish-speaking learners see 'What does he do?' and 'He is a doctor' in their written form first, they are likely to say /does/ instead of /dʌz/ and /dok'tor/ instead of /'doktə/. This is often called *spelling pronunciation*.

However, there are exceptions to this order of presentation. A reading text may be used to help establish the initial presentation context, especially at higher levels when spelling pronunciation is no longer a problem. And written texts will be used extensively when the goal of the course is focused principally on reading and/or writing skills.

Writing for clarification and consolidation

When the written form is presented, it can be used to clarify and consolidate the oral presentation and practice. This is especially important for those learners who are more visually oriented. If they know from your regular system of teaching that they will soon see the written form, this will reduce any anxiety they may have during oral presentation and practice.

Teaching idea

- A useful technique for relating the written form to normal pronunciation is eliciting oral examples from the learners, writing them on the board, and getting learners to read them aloud, maintaining the same pronunciation as in the oral practice. The written examples can then be used to clarify the grammar. Marks such as underlining and arrows (preferably in a different colour) can be used for this purpose, for example, with the Present Simple:

He singS   romantic ballads.
    ↓
He doeS not sing   rock.
(doesn't)

The model can then be converted into a simple fill-in exercise for learners to copy and complete:

1 He _____ romantic ballads.
2 He _____ _____ _____ rock.

The learners will then have written examples of the new item to study at home.

From presentation to practice

There is no clear dividing line between presentation and practice. Presentation normally develops into practice, often quite naturally. This can be seen in part of Extract 3 from the lesson we discussed previously:

Teacher	Good . . . she's writing a report in the space shuttle. And what is the space shuttle doing?
Learner 4	It's orbiting the earth.
Teacher	OK! So, Vicky's writing a report. What about the others? Rocky? Mm, what's this? A hamburger? What's Rocky doing? Anyone?
Learner 5	Rocky is eat a hamburger.
Teacher	Pardon, Eric? Eat?
Learner 5	Er . . . **Rocky's eating a hamburger.**
Teacher	Very good! What about Marc? Ah, this is a coffee, right. What's Marc doing? Anyone?
Learner 6	**Marc's drinking a coffee.**
Teacher	That's right! And Yuri?
Learner 7	**Yuri's sleeping.**

The teacher elicits models the class has already repeated, and then he elicits new models 'created' by the learners themselves. This is the beginning of practice. We will look at language practice in more detail in Chapter 3.

In the early stages of practice, it is often necessary to move backwards and forwards between practice and presentation, for example, with question – answer (Q–A) combinations. In the lesson we examined above, the teacher handled the Q–A combination:

What's _____ doing?
He/ she/ it's _____ing . . .

in the following stages:

Presentation of A (Extract 2) →
Practice (Extract 2) →
Presentation of Q (Extract 3) →
Practice (Extract 3) →
Practice of Q–A (Extract 3)

This procedure could also be described in terms of who asks and who answers—the teacher (T) or the learner (L):

TQ–LA → LQ–TA → LQ–LA

While the learners were practising answers (TQ–LA) in Extract 3 they were listening and responding to the teacher's questions, so they became quite familiar with them. The teacher simply needs to clarify the interrogative form and function when moving from practice of the answer to presentation of the question, and LQ–TA, then LQ–LA:

Extract 4

Teacher	Right. What's Yuri doing? What's Yuri doing? Eating, sleeping, writing? Sonia?
Learner	He's sleeping.
Teacher	Yes. Now listen to the question: What's Yuri doing? What—IS—Yuri—do—ING? What—IS . . . What's . . . Yuri do—ING . . . doing . . . What's Yuri doing? What's Yuri DOing? Repeat, everyone.
Learners	What's Yuri doing?
Teacher	Again.
Learners	What's Yuri doing?
Teacher	Good. Ask me the question, David.
Learner	What's Yuri doing?
Teacher	He's sleeping. A different question, Ana . . . about Vicky, or Marc, or . . .
Learner	What's Vicky doing?

Teacher	She's writing a report. A different question, Mario.
Learner	What's Rocky doing?
Teacher	You answer, Eric.
Learner	He's drink . . . no, eating a hamburger. He's eating a hamburger.

The lesson has moved from practice to presentation and back to practice again. It is rather artificial and mechanical practice, but even this kind of practice can be useful in many teaching situations, for example, with large groups.

Summary

In Chapter 2 we have considered the following points:

New items in an English language course. New language items are prominent in most courses. They may be functional, grammatical, or lexical items, and are usually thematically connected in a unit. Teachers need to know, and learners to learn, the meaning, use in communication, pronunciation, spelling, structure, and relevant grammar of new items. The major new items are usually presented in some kind of functional-grammatical combination. The emphasis may be more on the interactional aspect of the functional item (for example, greeting, introducing, apologizing), or on the notional aspect (for example, time, place). In this book we call them functional-grammatical items.

Presenting new functional-grammatical items. To organize efficient and effective presentation and practice of new items, you need to understand them well and plan with your own specific learners in mind, not just 'teach the book'. Some functional-grammatical items are more difficult because of their meaning and use, others because of their structure and grammar. You should be prepared to deal with both kinds of difficulty. Most functional-grammatical items are best presented through model sentences in an appropriate context or situation. You can often establish the context or situation fairly conversationally, virtually as part of the communicative work in the course. A practical general procedure is:

Establish context → Present key model/s → Check understanding

The place of writing in presentation. In the above procedure, the written form would normally be introduced after oral presentation and practice. In some cases, for example, where the course focuses on reading and/or writing skills, earlier introduction of the written form is appropriate. Writing can be used to clarify grammar, and to give learners a permanent record of the new item and its structure and grammar.

From presentation to practice. Presentation normally develops naturally into practice without a marked division between the stages. Sometimes a lesson goes backwards and forwards between practice and presentation, for example, when dealing with question–answer (Q–A) combinations.

Project

Planning a presentation

Purpose: to develop an awareness of how to help your learners learn new items.

Procedure:

1 In an international coursebook, examine some of the sections of material for the presentation of new functional-grammatical items.

2 Select one of these sections where you think the material is not entirely suitable for your learners (or the learners you hope to teach), for example, specific problems of meaning, use, or grammar are not taken into account, or the situation/topic is confusing or not of much interest for your learners.

3 Referring to the points on page 19, analyse the new item with your learners in mind, and plan an alternative presentation session. Prepare the necessary material.

4 Ask other teachers or trainee teachers to give you their opinion of your plan. If possible, teach the plan, and evaluate the results.

3 ORGANIZING LANGUAGE PRACTICE

Introduction

In this chapter we look at ways in which learners can begin to produce and use new language items. Practice may emphasize formal accuracy or communicative fluency. In accuracy practice, errors are usually dealt with immediately, but, as much as possible, the teacher helps the learners to correct themselves. In fluency practice, errors are not usually corrected during activities, although the teacher may bring some errors to the learners' attention afterwards. Written practice can also focus on accuracy or fluency. It is important to realize that presentation and practice of specific new items is only the beginning of the learning process. A great deal of communicative use, clarification, and remedial work are usually necessary to complete the learning of a language item or system.

The difference between accuracy and fluency practice

The presentation and practice of new language items is a major part of most English language courses, but you should not forget the main goal of English language teaching—to enable learners to use English effectively in real communication. Some kind of context should normally be provided for the new items when you first present them. Presentation usually develops naturally into practice, and the context often means the practice has at least an element of communication.

Presentation and practice have some specific objectives that are not in themselves communicative. In presentation, we expect learners to grasp how new items are structured and pronounced, as well as what they mean and how they are used in communication. The objectives of practice include enabling learners to recognize, pronounce, and manipulate new language items with some degree of subconscious automaticity. In other words, after practice, we want them to be able to make statements or ask and answer questions without always painfully constructing each sentence word by word.

Practice and communication

To promote automaticity, practice usually includes some repetition of new language items. However, organized repetition can be only the very beginning of the learning process. Repetition in the sense of 'repeated use in communication' is much more important. Repetition practice of new items often produces very unnatural discourse. Did anyone outside an English language classroom ever have a 'conversation' like this?

> **A** Is there a chair in your bedroom?
> **B** Yes, there is. Is there a table in your bedroom?
> **A** No, there isn't. Is there a television in your bedroom?
> **B** No, there isn't. Is there a mirror in your bedroom?

But this practice is more communicative than getting learners to say things like 'There's a blackboard in this classroom'. The learners are at least exchanging real information about their bedrooms while repeating the structures again and again.

This kind of practice activity could be made even more communicative if each learner had to find someone else with a specific item at home (for example, a computer, a bicycle, or a washing machine), and also some extra information about the item (for example, where it is kept, its age, or its make). This would mean the practice would require the use of more than just one structure or set of structures, for example:

> **A** Is there a computer in your house?
> **B** No, there isn't. Is there a washing machine in your house?
> **A** No, there isn't. Sorry. [*A and B look for other people to ask.*] Is there a computer in your house?
> **C** Yes, there is.
> **A** Ah, good! Where is it?
> **C** In my father's . . . er . . . *estudio.*
> **A** Um . . . study. How old is it?

A distinction is often made between *accuracy practice* and *fluency practice.* Accuracy practice is intended to establish some correctness in the production of new items immediately after they are presented, or to correct errors later on. Fluency practice is intended to get the learners to use new items in more natural communication. In accuracy practice, learners are usually very aware that they are repeating the new item or items over and over again. They also know that they are expected to avoid errors. However, this does not mean that after accuracy practice they will always produce and use the new items correctly in real conversations. Anyone with experience of learning, using, or teaching a foreign language knows that errors persist. In fluency practice you should try to get the learners' attention off the language and onto the communication of ideas. Repetition, or repeated use, of the new items is important, but it should be naturally combined with other language in communication. This means there may be more errors in fluency practice than in accuracy practice, but you should not normally interrupt learners to correct errors. Some teachers and learners feel unhappy with this tolerance of errors, but it is simply what will happen when learners use English outside the classroom. Errors in foreign language learning cannot be avoided.

Questions

Can you guess which of the four class extracts below are probably intended as accuracy practice and which as fluency practice? Why?

Extract 1

Learner 1	Have you ever been to Prague?
Learner 2	No I haven't. Have you?
Learner 1	Yes. It's wonderful.
Learner 2	How long did you stayed?
Learner 1	One week.
Learner 2	The buildings are beautiful, yes?
Learner 1	Yes, and the streets . . . the river . . .
Learner 2	Ah. Have you ever been in Rome?

Extract 2

Learner 1	Is the Neon bigger than the Chevy?
Learner 2	Yes, it is. Is the Lexus cheap than . . .
Teacher	Cheap . . . ?
Learner 2	Is the Lexus cheaper than the Chevy?
Learner 3	No, it isn't. Is the Lexus faster than the Neon?
Learner 4	Yes, it is. Is prettier the Neon . . .
Teacher	Is the . . .

Extract 3

Learner 1	My TV is three years old.
Learner 2	My TV is one hundred years old.
Teacher	Really?
Learner 2	No—but it is very old.
Teacher	Ah, I see! And your TV, Alex?
Learner 3	My TV has two years old.

Teacher	My TV . . .
Learner 3	. . . is two years old.
Teacher	Right. Ana. How old is your TV?

Extract 4

Learner 1	Hello. My name's John Smith.
Learner 2	Pleased to meet you. I'm Mary Swift.
Learner 1	Where are you from, Mary?
Learner 2	Ireland. And you?
Learner 1	I'm from Australia. What you do?
Learner 2	I'm a doctor. What do you do?
Learner 1	Chef. What are you doing in Paris?
Learner 2	I'm visiting a friend. And you?
Learner 1	I'm study French.

Extracts 1 and 4 have a lot in common, as do Extracts 2 and 3. In Extracts 1 and 4, the exchanges are between two learners only, probably working in pairs. Extract 4 is probably a *role play*, the learners pretending to be John Smith and Mary Swift. In these two extracts there are no interventions by the teacher. The language is varied, and there are a number of uncorrected errors (for example, *'How long did you stay*ed?', *'What you do?', and *'I'm study French.'). In Extracts 2 and 3, on the other hand, more learners are involved, probably because it is whole-class work. The teacher intervenes to get correction of errors. The language is highly repetitive (for example, 'Is the _____ _____ er than the _____ ?', 'My _____ is _____ years old.' There is some repetition of certain forms in Extracts 1 and 4 too—among other things, the learners in Extract 1 are practising the Present Perfect, and those in Extract 4 the Present Progressive—but it is less obvious. In fact, Extracts 1 and 4 are intended as fluency practice, and Extracts 2 and 3 as accuracy practice.

Oral accuracy practice

Oral accuracy practice involves the repetition of a language pattern or patterns, for example, 'My watch was made in Japan', 'My shoes were made in Italy'.

Language patterns and substitution

Repetition in accuracy practice is based on the principle of substitution in a pattern. A sentence or phrase pattern can be seen as a structure with both fixed elements and open spaces where many different elements can be inserted. The fixed and the substitutable elements in the above example are:

Pattern: My _____ _____ made in _____ .

The same principle can be applied to virtually any sentence or phrase pattern, for example:

What does _____ do?
      Sting
      Nicole

_____ is a/an _____ .
He   singer.
She   actress.

This kind of practice is often called a *drill* or *drilling*, because it can be very mechanical, like an army training exercise. It was the main kind of practice in the Audiolingual Method (see Chapter 12). But nowadays language drills are not considered so fundamental or beneficial in language teaching. However, they are still widely used in some form or other, especially for accuracy practice of new items, and in large groups. Most trained teachers today prefer to use drills only for short periods in their lessons, and they also try to make them as meaningful and attractive as possible for the learners.

Accuracy practice and communication

Accuracy practice does not have to be totally mechanical. By organizing it within an appropriate context or situation, you can make it attractive and meaningful for your learners. Sometimes the language can be used in quite a communicative way.

Questions

Which of the three accuracy practice class extracts below do you think is most unnatural and non-communicative, and which do you think is most natural and communicative? Why?

Extract 5

Teacher	Where was the Mercedes made, Samuel?
Learner 1	It was made in Germany.
Teacher	Right. Where was the Ferrari made, Ana?
Learner 2	It made in Italy.
Teacher	It . . . ?
Learner 2	It . . . was . . . made in Italy.
Teacher	Good. It was made in Italy. Where was the Buick made, Roberto?
Learner 3	It was made in the USA.
Teacher	Right. Where was the Jaguar made, Laura?

Extract 6

Teacher	Watch—Japan. Yuri.
Learner 1	The watch was made in Japan.
Teacher	Good. Shoes—Italy. Raisa.
Learner 2	The shoes was . . . were made in Italy.
Teacher	Mm . . . Again.
Learner 2	. . . The shoes were made in Italy.
Teacher	OK Calculator—China. Boris.
Learner 3	The calculator was made in China.
Teacher	Car—USA. Elena.

Extract 7

Teacher	OK, check your watches, calculators, pens …
Learner 1	Our shoes, teacher? Our bag?
Teacher	Sure. Why not? OK, let's see how free trade is affecting us. What about your watch, Samuel?
Learner 2	My watch was made in Japan.
Teacher	Ah, a Citizen like mine. What about your shoes, Lucy?
Learner 3	They my shoes … No? … They … were made in Italy.
Teacher	Good. They're nice. What about your bag, Ana?
Learner 4	It was made in Portugal.
Teacher	Portugal? Really? Where was your pen made, Luis?

All three teachers get the learners to repeat the new pattern over and over again, substituting elements in the structure. They all use techniques to *elicit*—in other words, obtain—responses from the learners and control the practice. But the techniques and manner of the teachers differ greatly. The teacher in Extract 5 uses the question pattern 'Where was the _____ made?' every time. The teacher in Extract 6 uses two-word *cues* (for example, 'watch—Japan') every time. The teacher in Extract 7 uses the question pattern 'What about your _____ ?' several times, and then moves to the pattern 'Where was your _____ made?'

On a scale from unnatural/non-communicative to natural/communicative, Extracts 5, 6, and 7 might be classified something like this:

Unnatural/non-communicative ◄────────► Natural/communicative

6   5   7

The most unnatural/non-communicative practice is in Extract 6. The teacher gets the learners to produce sentences by using the artificial cue 'object–country', for example, 'Watch–Japan'. And she does not learn any new information from the learners' answers. The most natural/communicative practice is in Extract 7. The teacher uses questions as cues, for example, 'What about your shoes' and 'Where was your pen made?' She learns real, new information from the learners' answers about where their possessions were made. And she responds with conversational comments, for example, 'They're nice'. Extract 5 comes somewhere in between. The teacher uses questions rather than cues, but there is no variation in them. The learners answer with information known to the teacher, and the teacher makes no conversational comments.

Many teachers nowadays would rarely use the type of practice in Extract 6, and would not use the type of practice in Extract 5 much. They would try to use something like the type of practice in Extract 7, even in accuracy work. Most recent research and theory in foreign language learning supports this approach. Truly successful learning of a foreign language seems to be the result principally of practising the language by communicating with it.

However, many successful learners feel that the mechanical drilling they did in classes did help them when they eventually tried to use the language for real communication. While natural, communicative repetition practice, like that in Extract 7, is probably best in general, even very mechanical drills may be useful, for example to work on pronunciation and grammar in large groups. Mechanical drills are more enjoyable for the learners if the topic is attractive for them, for example, animals for children, pop stars for teenagers, and famous bridges and dams for civil engineering students. Attractive presentation also helps, for example, pictures or real objects such as those in Extracts 6 and 7. (Real objects used as teaching aids are often referred to as *realia*.) Drills are also more effective if handled in a brisk, lively, cheerful way, rather than a monotonous, boring, severe way. Communicative repetition practice, on the other hand, tends to be slower and more relaxed. The learners may have to think a little about the information they are communicating.

Information gaps

Communicative accuracy practice requires some form of *information gap*. This is when one speaker knows information the other speaker does not. In Extract 7, the learners know where their possessions were made, but the teacher does not. When the teacher asks 'Where was your pen made, Luis?' she does not know the answer, so there is some communication. In contrast, the teacher in Extract 5 does know the answer to the question 'Where was the Jaguar made?' because it is on the board. There is no information gap, and therefore no communication. In Extract 7 the teacher's question is a real one seeking information, while in Extract 5 it is a *display question*. This is the type of artificial practice question that teachers ask in classes, but people do not ask in normal conversations.

Teaching ideas

• Get your learners to work in pairs and ask each other questions like the following:
  Is there a chair/mirror/television/etc. in your bedroom?
  What time do you get up/have breakfast/leave home/etc.?
  How old is your television/watch/jacket etc.?
  Have you ever eaten iguana/drunk cactus juice/seen a dolphin/etc.?

• Artificial information gaps can be created by giving some learners one set of information and other learners different information. This is usually done in pairwork. Here are two examples of information gap material for accuracy practice in pairs:

Starlight Inn	
Rooms:	85
Suites:	
Pools:	2
Restaurants:	
Bars:	2
Conference rooms:	

Starlight Inn	
Rooms:	
Suites:	4
Pools:	
Restaurants:	3
Bars:	
Conference rooms:	5

Card A   *Card B*

Each learner looks at only one card and completes it by asking questions like:

    A How many rooms are there in the hotel?
    B There are eighty-five. How many swimming pools are there?
    A There are two. How many . . . ?

One learner looks only at Picture A and the other learner only at Picture B. They practise like this, noting which animals they have in both their petshops:

    A Is there a cat in your petshop?
    B Yes, there is. Is there a dog in your petshop?
    A No, there isn't. Is there a . . . ?

You can also organize interaction in groups and between groups (or rows, or teams). An appropriate use of a range of interactions can make lessons much more dynamic than the 'traditional' continuously T→L lesson. Even in accuracy practice you should use as wide a range of interactions as possible.

Elicitation in accuracy practice

If you teach in a context where you need to do a lot of mechanical drilling, try to make it brisk and lively. Effective *cues* and *nomination* of learners are vital. Types of cue that elicit specific sentences from learners quickly include:

- Words—for example, 'watch—Japan', spoken, or written on cards which you hold up.
- Realia—for example, a watch, perhaps with a country of origin label or tag to elicit 'It was made in _____ '.
- Flashcards—for example, pictures of objects.
- Questions—for example, 'Where was the _____ made?', perhaps with a poster of cars and countries.
- Gesture/mime—for example, mime swimming to elicit 'You're swimming'.
- Statements—'You want a drink' to elicit 'I'm thirsty'.

The nomination of learners should be clear, and usually unpredictable. You can use:

- Names—after the cue so all the learners are ready to respond, for example, 'Watch—Japan. Yuri?'
- A polite gesture of the hand indicating the learner—again, after the cue.
- Row numbers or group names for choral responses—for example, 'Row two!' or 'Eagles!'

It is best to nominate the learner, or learners, *after* giving the cue so that all of them remain attentive and ready to respond. Nominating unpredictably in different places round the class rather than in a predictable sequence along a row tends to have the same effect. Your smile and enthusiastic manner can also contribute to the liveliness of a drill.

For more communicative practice, instead of obvious cues you can use conversational questions or requests for information, for example, 'What about your watch?', or 'Where was your calculator made?' 'What about _____ ?' and 'Tell me about _____ ' are very versatile elicitation cues. They can be used to elicit almost any statement pattern. For example, 'What about your watch?' or 'Tell me about your watch' could elicit 'It *was made* in Japan', or 'It's *Japanese*', or 'It's *two years old*', according to which pattern you are practising.

Interactions

Extracts 5, 6, and 7 are all Teacher → Learner (T→L) interactions. Apart from choral repetition and choral responses to teacher questions or cues (T→LL), this is probably the commonest interaction pattern in most classrooms. But classroom interaction need not always follow these patterns. It can be quite varied, and consequently more interesting for learners. It can also be more like conversation outside the classroom. For example, the teacher can prompt one learner to ask another a question, or learners can be given questionnaires and told to ask each other questions.

Topics and activities

All language practice should be organized as far as possible around topics of interest to the learners. This is true of items that can best be seen in functional terms (for example, making requests or giving directions) and of items best seen in structural terms (for example, talking about the past). With younger children, making requests or giving directions are much better practised in the context of Disneyland rather than that of banks, hotels, and restaurants in a city. With sociology students, the Past Tense is much better practised talking about life in the 1950s than a day in the life of Mickey Mouse. Varied activities, interactions and topics can all contribute to making oral accuracy practice, and lessons in general, more enjoyable and effective for the learners.

Teaching ideas

- Get the learners to make statements in response to your cues, for example:

Teacher	Singers, Ana.
Learner 1	I like Maria Carey and Elton John.
Teacher	TV programmes, David.
Learner 2	I like . . .

- Get the learners to answer your questions, for example:

Teacher	Where was your watch made?
Learner	It was made in the Philippines.

- Get the learners to ask and answer questions in pairs, for example:

Learner 1	Which composer do you like most, Alicia?
Learner 2	I like John Lennon. Which singer do you like most, Guille?
Learner 3	I like Sting. Which . . .

- Get the learners to ask you questions, for example:

Learner 1	What animals do you like?
Teacher	I like cats.
Learner 2	What sports do you like?
Teacher	I like . . .

- Use chain drills. For example, to practise the 'Going to' future, get each learner to repeat what the previous learners said and add another sentence:

Learner 1	This weekend, I'm going to swim.
Learner 2	This weekend, Ana is going to swim. I'm going to study.
Learner 3	This weekend Ana is going to swim. David is going to study. I'm going to . . .

- Use 'find-someone-who' surveys. For example, to practise 'can', get the learners to mingle and ask different classmates 'Can you _____ ?' questions in order to complete a form like this as quickly as possible:

Ability	Student's name
play the piano	
dance the mambo	
drive a car	

- Use team games and competitions such as noughts-and-crosses. To practise the Superlative, get Team A and Team B to take turns making true statements using the adjectives in the squares, for example, 'Everest is the highest mountain in the world' or 'New York is the most important city in America'. If the sentence is correct, the team wins the square with the adjective in it. The first team to win three squares in a straight row wins the game.

1 long	2 important	3 powerful
4 economical	5 high	6 good
7 fast	8 bad	9 expensive

Oral fluency practice

The main objective of oral accuracy practice is to get learners to begin to produce formally correct versions of new items. In oral fluency practice, the main objective is to get them to use the items in conversations and other communication without hesitation, even if they make mistakes. Their attention should be more on the information they are communicating than on the language. Oral fluency work should continue if possible into free conversations (see Chapter 5), but we will restrict our attention here to fluency practice intended to consolidate the learning of specific language items.

Accuracy practice typically involves using only the new items. Fluency practice, on the other hand, usually combines them with other language. Because of this emphasis on communication and on the more natural use of language, the choice of topics, activities, and types of interaction are even more important in fluency practice than in accuracy practice.

Types of fluency activity

In order to ensure some use of recently introduced items in fluency practice the learners must be guided in some way. This may be through a model text or script, or through visual or other materials.

Script-based activities

Extracts 1 and 4 (see pages 37–9) are examples of oral fluency practice activities that are based on a model text or script. The learners are working in pairs, and they make some mistakes, just as they would if they were having a real conversation outside the classroom. However, the practice probably started with an accurate model or script, and as *lockstep* work supervised directly by the teacher.

When handling such activities, it is best to move systematically from accuracy to fluency work in the following stages:

1 Establish a model, for example, use a cassette recording, or build up a dialogue with the help of the learners. Then do some choral and individual repetition of sections of the dialogue, or the whole dialogue, and indicate possible substitutions.

2 Act out the dialogue with one of the learners, changing some information, that is, substituting parts of the original dialogue.

3 Get the learners to work in pairs, modifying the original dialogue according to the personal or other information they are communicating. You could also get the learners to switch partners. Circulate among the pairs monitoring in order to help if necessary, and noting errors that will need attention after the fluency practice.

Here is an illustration of the way Extract 1 could be set up and developed according to these stages:

Stage 1

Teacher	OK. Look at this picture. What is it?

Learner 1	Party . . . it's a party.
Teacher	That's right. It's a party, or a reception. What are the people doing?
Learner 2	They're drinking.
Teacher	Yes, and . . .
Learner 3	They're speaking.
Teacher	Right. They're talking. Now listen to this conversation at the party.

[Teacher plays the following conversation on the coursebook cassette]

Man: It's a nice party.
Woman: Er . . . yes, it is.
Man: Hello. My name's John Smith.
Woman: Pleased to meet you. I'm Mary Swift.
Man: Where are you from, Mary?
Woman: Dublin, Ireland. And you?
Man: I'm from Perth, Australia. What do you do?
Woman: I'm a doctor. What about you?
Man: I'm a chef. What are you doing here in Paris, Mary?
Woman: I'm visiting a friend. And you?
Man: I'm studying French.
Woman: Oh, excuse me—that's my friend, Pierre. Nice talking to you, John.
Man: Oh . . . sure . . . nice talking to you.

Teacher	No problems? *[Teacher stops the cassette.]* Good. Let's check. Where's the party?
Learner 4	In Paris.
Teacher	What's the man's name?
Learner 5	John Smith. *[Teacher asks more comprehension questions: the woman's name, where they are from, what they are doing in Paris. Teacher plays the cassette again.]*
Teacher	Now, let's check your memory. The man starts. He says: It's a . . .
Learner 2	. . . a nice party.
Teacher	Good. It's a nice party. It's a nice party. Everyone.
Learners	It's a nice party.
Teacher	The woman answers. She says . . .
Learner 6	Yes, it is.

[Teacher goes through the key expressions in the dialogue this way.]

Stage 2

Teacher	Now, I want a volunteer. Ana? Good. OK, Ana, we're at the party, in Paris. Look at the information on this card for a moment. OK?
Learner 1	Yes.
Teacher	Do you understand the information? It's your information, OK?
Learner 1	Yes.
Teacher	Right. Uhum . . . It's a nice party.
Learner 1	Yes, it is.
Teacher	Hello. I'm Hans Schiller.
Learner 1	Pleased to meet you. My name's Yoko Matsumoto.
Teacher	Where are you from, Yoko?
Learner 1	I'm from Kyoto, Japan. And you?
Teacher	I'm from Vienna, Austria. What you do?
Learner 1	I'm a graphic designer. What do you do?
Teacher	I'm an actor. What are you doing here in Paris, Yoko?
Learner 1	I'm attending a conference. And you?
Teacher	I'm making a film.
Learner 1	Nice talking to you. That's my husband. He's a karate instructor.
Teacher	Oh! Nice talking to you . . . Very good, Ana! *[Teacher turns to class.]* OK, so what's her name?
Learner 2	Yoko Matsumoto.
Teacher	What does she do?
Learner 3	She's a graphic designer.

Teacher	And what's she doing in Paris?
Learner 4	She's attend . . . she's attending a conference.
Teacher	Good. She's attending a conference . . . a designers' conference, I imagine. Let's consider different reasons for visiting Paris. What about John Smith? He's . . .
Learner 5	Studying French.
Teacher	Right—he's studying French. And Mary Swift?
Learner 6	She's visiting a friend.

[Teacher goes through 'visiting', 'studying', 'attending', 'making a film', and elicits more possibilities from the learners, for example— 'touring Europe', 'doing a master's degree', 'working in a French company'.]

Stage 3

Teacher	OK. Take a card—blue cards for the men, pink cards for the women. Memorize the information. *[The teacher allows a few minutes for this.]* Now, I want two volunteers. Good. Come up here to the front. Where are you now?
Learner 1	At the front.
Teacher	No, no . . . you're at a . . .
Learner 2	. . . party . . . in Paris.
Teacher	Yes! OK, so . . . make conversation!

[The two learners act out a new conversation. When they finish, the teacher gets them to separate, and then gets two more volunteers to come to the front and start new conversations with each of the first two volunteers.]

Teacher	Very good. Now everybody stand up. Where are you?
Learners	At a party in Paris!
Teacher	Right! Where are your drinks? That's better. Now, make conversation!

[The learners all converse. The teacher walks around listening, after a while getting pairs to finish their conversations, separate, and open a new conversation with another partner. Finally the teacher gets the learners to stop talking and sit down.]

Teacher	Well, that was a great party. Any interesting people? Yes?
Learner 3	Yes. *[Learner 3 points to another learner.]*
Teacher	Oh, yes? Tell us about her.
Learner 3	Her name's Karen Okumba. She's from Kenya. She's an engineer, and she's competing in the Paris Marathon.

[The teacher checks some more information, and then gets the learners to write about two or three of the people they met at the party.]

These or similar stages, modified for the specific activity and group, can be used with most activities that are script-based. Apart from simulated social interactions such as the cocktail party in the example, these can include simulated practical transactions such as a dialogue between a customer and a shop assistant, and conversations about real personal experiences and ideas such as a memorable holiday, or predictions for the twenty-first century. The cocktail party provides practice of the Present Progressive, with contrast of 'What do you do?' and 'What are you doing?' This fluency activity can be repeated from time to time during the course with the learners incorporating new language items in more extended conversations, for example, 'Are you married?' and 'Have you been to Paris before?'

Unscripted activities

Apart from using a base script, learners can be guided towards the use of specific new language items in fluency activities with other materials. These may be pictures, questionnaires, forms, or notes. Here are some examples.

Teaching ideas

- Get learners in groups of three or four; take turns in saying something about these countries—for example, 'I think it's New Zealand', 'I think the capital is Sydney', 'I think the weather's cold'.

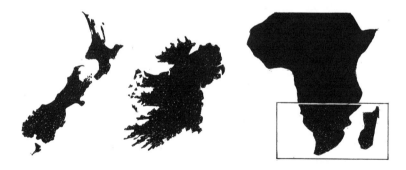

The other learners respond with expressions like 'Yes, I agree', or 'I don't think so. I think the capital is Wellington.' At first, they may be very conscious of the expressions they are using, but they should begin to forget about them as they get involved in discussion. They may even stop using the expressions and simply say things like 'It's Ireland', and 'Yes'. If they do this, as you monitor you should prompt with questions like 'Are you absolutely sure?' and 'Do you agree?'

- Get learners to interview one another about cities they would like to visit, and complete a form:

Cities	Reasons why	What you would do there
1		
2		

The learner interviewing could begin: 'What city would you most like to visit for a week?' The learner being interviewed would need to use 'I'd …' in answering the third column, but also a variety of other language forms in answering the second column. This activity could be organized as a survey to discover the two most popular cities for the whole class, the reasons why, and what people would do in those cities.

- Learner A has a biography form to complete with sections headed Name, Place of birth, Date of birth, Life and work, etc. Learner B has the biographical notes from an encyclopedia entry about a famous person, for example:

Van Gogh, Vincent, born Holland, 1853, sombre early social paintings, bright dynamic paintings after moving to France in 1886, many years in mental asylums, died 1890, suicide.

Learner A asks Learner B questions and completes the form. The learners would use many Past Tense forms in this activity.

Both types of guided fluency activity—script-based and unscripted—are included in most coursebooks. Whether you use book activities or design your own, you need to handle them in careful stages as described on page 48 for script-based activities.

Feedback and correction in oral practice

So far in this chapter we have focused on the principles and practice of getting learners to produce specific language items in accuracy work and then in fluency work. In the process, we have also seen many examples of how teachers may respond to the learners' efforts. Naturally, the way you give feedback and correction should be different in accuracy work, when the emphasis is on the language forms, and in fluency work, when the emphasis is on effective and hesitation-free communication.

Feedback and correction in accuracy work

In Extracts 2 and 3, on page 39–40, the learners are doing accuracy practice and the teacher is correcting them. The approaches of the two teachers are very different. The teacher in Extract 2 focuses exclusively on the language, while the teacher in Extract 3 responds to the communicative content with comments like 'Really?' But they have one important thing in common: they do not themselves correct the learners' errors—they help the learners to self-correct. It is a common assumption among teachers—and learners—that it is the teacher's job to correct learners, and that learners cannot correct themselves. Neither assumption is true. But it is true that learners will be passive and not correct themselves if you continually do it for them, and also that learners must eventually correct themselves if they are really to learn the language. The trick for teachers is to get learners used to self-correcting, and to give them help when necessary.

There are specific techniques for helping learners to self-correct. In Extracts 2 and 3, three different techniques are used:

– Repeating the incorrect form with a questioning intonation (for example, 'Cheap . . . ?').
– Giving the correct form or the beginning of it, but not the whole sentence (for example, 'Is the Lexus . . . ').
– Repeating the sentence up to the error (for example, 'My TV . . . ').

In each case, the teacher then waits for the learner to self-correct. If the learner fails to self-correct, more help is needed. There are many other techniques for providing help with self-correction, for example:

– Simply indicate an error with a questioning facial expression, or say 'Sorry?'
– Move one hand over the other for wrong word order.
– Point backwards or forwards for past or future tense.
– Give the learner a choice—'Cheap . . . cheaper . . . more cheap?'
– Draw an S in the air with a finger for errors like *'He live in Rome'.

Many correction techniques used by teachers are ingenious but quite intuitive. The important thing is that they should be appropriate for the specific error and clear for the learners. It is important always to use the same set of techniques so that learners can become familiar with them.

In accuracy practice, most errors in key features of the new item should normally be corrected immediately, but:

1 You should first give learners the opportunity to correct themselves, helping as necessary (*self-correction*).
2 If a learner cannot self-correct, you should invite other learners to make the correction (*peer correction*).

3 If no other learner can make the correction, you should make the correction yourself (*teacher correction*).

Remember, though, that speaking and making errors in a foreign language with the rest of the class looking and listening makes most learners nervous. You should consider the learners' sensitivities as well as your language teaching objectives. That means, for example, that you should not insist and insist on self-correction until the learner wants to disappear through the floor. Also, peer correction should be handled sensitively: for example, do not always call on the same 'good' learners to correct the same 'weak' ones. If self- and peer-correction fail, and you eventually have to make the correction yourself, it may mean something went seriously wrong in the earlier stages of the lesson, and some aspect of your presentation may need to be repeated.

In Extracts 2 and 3, there is also feedback from the teachers that is not corrective, for example, 'Good' in Extract 2, and 'Really?', 'Ah, I see', and 'Right' in Extract 3. Always indicating when a learner's utterance is correct, for example, with 'Good', may make learners focus too much on linguistic correctness, and reduce their willingness later to engage in real communication. Many learners do seem reluctant to speak freely, or at all, because they are afraid of making mistakes. It is probably best to accustom them to the general rule that an utterance is satisfactory unless you indicate otherwise. Indications that an utterance is linguistically correct can then be reserved for cases like 'Right' in Extract 3, when the learner has successfully corrected himself. Responses to *what* learners say, for example, 'Really?' and 'Ah, I see' in Extract 3, are positive because they tend to have the opposite effect. They encourage learners to communicate without being obsessed with linguistic correctness. The teacher in Extract 3 seems to be of that view, while the teacher in Extract 2 does not, at least in accuracy practice.

Feedback and correction in fluency work

When you decide to intervene to correct errors in fluency practice, the recommended self → peer → teacher correction sequence applies as in accuracy practice. But since fluency is about effective communication without much hesitation, you should not interrupt activities too often. Do so only when many learners are making the same basic error, or when errors interfere with communication. Instead, monitor the activity, note common errors, and deal with them after the activity has finished. One way of doing this is to write sentences with significant errors in them on the board—without saying who made the errors. Then get the learners to identify and correct them.

Written practice

Like spoken practice, written practice may be oriented towards accuracy or fluency. It may be repetitive and controlled (for example, an exercise with ten Past Tense sentences to complete), or quite free (for example, a short composition about what learners did during the weekend, again probably producing several Past Tense sentences—but the learner's own).

Some teachers prefer to leave written practice until after extensive spoken practice in order to begin to establish good pronunciation and natural speech. Early reading and writing do often seem to interfere with natural speech and pronunciation. Learners may construct sentences word by word, and they may use 'spelling pronunciation'. However, some reading and writing during oral practice can be reassuring for visually or analytically oriented learners. It also provides a change of activity. In certain teaching–learning situations it may actually be appropriate to organize more reading and writing than spoken practice—for example, in courses with large groups where reading comprehension is the main objective, and time is short.

Teaching ideas

- In Chapter 2 we saw a simple fill-in exercise using sentences from oral practice:

  1 He _____ romantic ballads.
  2 He _____ rock.

  The second sentence here could be made easier, if the teacher thought it appropriate, by giving separate lines (_____ _____) for each of the two missing elements ('doesn't' and 'sing'). Also, just one of the two elements could be omitted ('doesn't ___ ', or ' _____ sing'). This kind of fill-in related to previous oral practice can be very useful as a first written exercise.

- Use multiple choice fill-ins, for example:
  He _____ sing rock.
  (a) don't (b) doesn't (c) not.

- Get the learners to write or complete answers, for example:
  What kind of songs does he sing? He _____ .

- Get the learners to write or complete questions, for example:
  What kind of _____ ? He sings romantic ballads.

- Get the learners to make sentences from scrambled words, for example:
  know songs you do what sings he of kind ?

- Get the learners to match divided sentences or questions or answers, for example:

  1 Rick Floss . . .   B . . . sing rock.
  2 He doesn't . . .   A . . . sings romantic ballads.

- When exercises like these focus on just one new grammatical structure or set of structures, they are appropriate only for early accuracy practice. For later written practice, different structures should be mixed as they are in real conversations, letters, and so on. In fact, a very common type of exercise for later written practice is dialogue or text completion:

Jack	Do you (1) _____ Rick Floss?
Jill	Yes, (2) _____ . In my opinion he's (3) _____ great singer.
Jack	But he doesn't (4) _____ rock. He only (5) _____ romantic ballads.
Jill	That's not true. He's very versatile. He (6) _____ sing anything.

Later written practice is also likely to include guided compositions (see Chapter 6). In fact, all the practice of the spoken and the written language discussed in this chapter should if possible develop into the skills development dealt with in Chapters 5 and 6.

Summary

In Chapter 3 we have considered the following points:

The difference between accuracy and fluency practice. Practice normally develops naturally out of presentation, and is related to a particular context or situation, which can give a communicative element. Language practice aims at getting some kind of repetition or repeated use of the same item(s). Early practice tends to focus on accuracy, later practice on fluency.

Oral accuracy practice. Accuracy practice is usually based on the substitution of elements in a pattern. Nowadays it is usually kept brief or given a communicative element, typically some form of information gap (one person knowing something the other does not). It may be more mechanical and extensive in large groups. Even then attractive topics and lively handling can make it fun, but effective cues and nomination of learners are vital. In general, varied topics, activities, and interactions (including pairwork) are important in accuracy practice.

Oral fluency practice. The learners' attention should now be more on the information they are communicating than on the language. Also, fluency practice usually combines new items with other language as preparation for the use of the new items in conversations, etc., without hesitation, even if with some errors. The language used may be guided by dialogue scripts or by materials such as pictures and forms, but information gap and some freedom for the learners to decide exactly what they say are essential in fluency practice.

Feedback and correction in oral practice. In accuracy work, most errors should be corrected immediately, but in fluency work they should usually be dealt with after the activity. In either case, when corrections are made, you should first try to elicit self-correction, and if that fails, peer correction. Teacher correction should be used only as a last resort. Communicative feedback (responding to *what* learners say) can encourage learners to speak and express their own ideas.

Written practice. This may often be left until after substantial oral practice, but some written work during oral practice can provide useful changes of activity and help and encourage visual and analytical learners. It can be accuracy oriented (for example, fill-ins with the new items only), or more fluency oriented (for example, dialogue completions).

Project

Analysing practice activities

Purpose: to develop an awareness of the nature of different practice materials and activities.

Procedure:

1 Examine all the oral practice materials/activities in one unit of a coursebook you are using or might use.
2 Classify each as mainly intended to develop accuracy (A) or fluency (F).
3 Classify each of the 'A' activities as totally mechanical (MM), rather mechanical (M), or fairly communicative (C). What kind of information gap does each 'C' activity have?
4 Decide what cues you would use for each 'A' activity, and how you would handle them if you decided to use them.
5 Decide what stages and steps you would follow for each 'F' activity.
6 Decide whether you would modify any of the activities. If so, what changes would you make, and why?

4 HANDLING VOCABULARY

Introduction

In this chapter we look at the importance of vocabulary in communication and the need to give it adequate attention in teaching. This involves more knowledge and skill than many teachers think. We suggest ways of dealing with the meaning, use in communication, pronunciation, spelling, and grammar of new words. Presentation and practice is just the beginning. We also suggest ways of reactivating and continuing to work on previously introduced vocabulary, including remedial work when necessary.

Vocabulary in language teaching and learning

In communication, vocabulary is often more important than grammar. It is frustrating for intermediate learners when they discover they cannot communicate effectively because they do not know many of the words they need. Unfortunately, vocabulary is neglected in some English language courses. This is a pity because working with words can be enjoyable and satisfying for learners.

That does not mean that learning words and how to use them is a simple matter. On the contrary, it is quite challenging. While grammar at least seems to be finite, vocabulary is virtually infinite. Words are also more complex than they appear to be on the surface. Amongst other things, they behave differently in different languages. For example, one word—*techo*—is used for 'roof' and 'ceiling' in Spanish, while two separate words—*jugar* and *tocar*—are used for the English word 'play' (referring respectively to playing a sport and playing a musical instrument).

Keeping hundreds, and later thousands, of words active and available for use is also difficult for classroom learners of a foreign language. Children acquiring their native language and immigrants acquiring an L2 learn new words as they encounter them and need them in life. Learning is consolidated by frequent and even daily use of the words in real communication. But learners in a classroom often have to make a special effort to memorize words that they seldom use in communication. It may sometimes seem to them that they need the words only for the next test. For this reason, teachers need to consider carefully what vocabulary to introduce in each lesson, and also how to reactivate previously introduced vocabulary. New words and expressions may be specified for each unit of your syllabus or coursebook—for example, in a 'new vocabulary' list or in the Teacher's Book. If not, you yourself will have to select appropriate vocabulary. Your selection of vocabulary should take the learners' interests and needs into account as well as the general topic of the lesson.

You may have to deal with new vocabulary at any time in your lessons. When you know that specific new words or expressions will be used in a lesson—for example, 'get up', 'take a shower', and 'have breakfast', when the topic of your lesson is 'talking about routine activities'—you can be fully prepared. You can also often anticipate that certain other items might be needed—for example, words for other routine activities which are not part of your lesson plan but which learners might want to talk about. But at other times, especially at higher levels, new words come up quite unexpectedly. Then you have to respond spontaneously. This may sometimes mean saying you are not absolutely sure about a word, but will investigate before the next lesson. This last point is important. Learners often expect teachers to know everything about their subject, and are critical if they do not. But it is dangerous to pretend you know absolutely everything. And you can easily demonstrate to learners that they do not know many regularly used words in their own language.

Dealing with new vocabulary

The aspects of new vocabulary items that you may need to know about and learners may need to learn are similar to those of other new language items such as grammatical patterns or functional expressions (see Chapter 2). Essentially, these aspects are meaning, use in communication, pronunciation and spelling, and grammar.

Meaning and use in communication

The meaning of new words and expressions can be presented through translation, in other words, giving an equivalent word or expression in the learners' native language. But there are several potential disadvantages to this technique. For example, it may encourage learners to think in their own language, always translating to and from English. Also, it may encourage learners to feel they have learnt a word or expression permanently once they have been given the translation. And it may give wrong ideas about a word or expression—for example, French *la politique* is equivalent to English 'politics', but it can also be equivalent to 'the politician' or 'the policy' in different contexts. Finally, it may lead to lengthy and perhaps confusing discussion in the learners' first language.

Of course, it is natural and useful to use translation from time to time, but it is important to avoid making it the usual way of presenting the meaning of new items. Most vocabulary items can be presented very clearly without translation. In fact, other techniques generally involve the learners more, and they remember better. Here are some examples of different ways of presenting vocabulary items:

Extract 1

Teacher	Mary bought a pair of shoes and a wallet. A wallet, OK? No? Well, this is my wallet—look. Have you got a wallet, Yuri? Ah, yes. Is it full of money?
Learner	No . . . it's nearly empty!
Teacher	Ah, like mine.

Extract 2

Teacher	Look at this picture. This is a knight, and this is a castle. A knight. A castle. What's this, David?
Learner 1	A knight.
Teacher	Right. And this, Rebecca?
Learner 2	A castle.
Teacher	Right. A knight and a castle.

Extract 3

Teacher	Kangaroos can jump ten metres. Can you jump, Stefan?
Learner	Yump?
Teacher	Yes, like this. [*The teacher demonstrates.*]
Learner	Oh, yes.
Teacher	Can you jump ten metres?
Learner	No!

Extract 4

Teacher	What's his name? No? Well, his name's Sting. He's a singer. Sting's a singer. A singer . . . Whitney Houston's a singer, and Michael Bolton, and . . . Come on, singers, names of singers . . .
Learner 1	Pavarotti.
Teacher	Yes! Pavarotti's an opera singer.
Learner 2	Madonna.
Teacher	Yes, she's a pop singer.

Extract 5

Teacher	She doesn't understand—she's a foreigner. A foreigner? No? A person from another country. Is Paul McCartney a foreigner when he's here in this country?
Learner 1	Yes.
Teacher	Is he a foreigner in the USA?
Learner 2	Yes.
Teacher	That's right. He isn't American. Is he a foreigner in England?
Learner 3	No—he's English.

Extract 6

Teacher	Look at the expression on her face. She's upset. What do you think 'upset' is in Spanish?
Learner 1	*Molesta?*
Teacher	Yes . . . more or less . . .
Learner 2	*Perturbada.*
Teacher	Right!

In these examples, meaning is presented with real objects (realia) (Extract 1), examples (Extract 4), pictures (Extract 2), definition (Extract 5), demonstration (Extract 3), translation (Extract 6). Realia, pictures, and demonstration are especially useful for presenting the concrete vocabulary of beginners' and elementary courses. Examples are often useful at these levels also. Definitions as well as examples are especially useful for the more abstract vocabulary of upper elementary and intermediate courses. Translation, as we have already said, is best used as a last resort. It is also best, when possible, to elicit the translation from a learner, as in Extract 6. Involving learners actively can motivate them and help them remember the item.

You can also present meaning with mime and gesture, for example, 'driving a car', or 'swimming'. Using contrast, or antonyms is another technique, for example, 'This building is ugly. It isn't beautiful—it's ugly. Ugly.' The opposite of using *antonyms* is using equivalence, or *synonyms*, for example, 'They're having a chat—a conversation.' Presenting the meaning of vocabulary items, avoiding translation as much as possible, is an opportunity for creativity and ingenuity in teaching.

An important point to note about the extracts above is that the vocabulary is presented in a context, not as isolated words. An appropriate context helps learners begin to understand the use of the item as well as its basic meaning. The item is associated with a certain type of context or situation. 'Upset', for example, is associated with people's feelings or reactions to events.

Another important point to note about the extracts is that the teacher usually checks that the learners have understood. For example, in Extract 1 the teacher gets a learner to show his own wallet, and in Extract 4, the teacher gets the learners to give more examples of singers. Note also that in Extracts 1 and 5 the teacher checks whether any learners already know the item— 'She doesn't understand—she's a foreigner. A foreigner? No?' Remember, there may be learners who do already know the item. Giving them the opportunity to show that knowledge can be motivating for them and set a good example of active participation for the whole group. This is especially true with false beginner and intermediate learners.

Pronunciation and spelling

Obviously, learners must be able to recognize and produce the form of a new vocabulary item as well as understand its meaning and use. They must learn how the new item is pronounced, and how it is written. It is usually best to present new items orally first and in written form later, especially at lower levels (see Chapter 2). The main advantage to this procedure when dealing with new vocabulary is that you can avoid learners getting into the habit of using 'spelling pronunciation'. For example, in a lesson on health problems, a teacher we observed was having trouble with the pronunciation of 'stomach ache'. The Mexican learners had seen the words written and they were fixed in their heads as /stomatʃ/ and /eitʃ/, rhyming with 'match' and the letter 'H'. The teacher gave lots of choral and individual repetition practice of the correct pronunciation—/stʌmək/ and /eɪk/, but the learners continually slipped back into spelling pronunciation. Eventually, he came up with a memorable idea:

Teacher	No, no. Listen—stomach-ache . . . um . . . cake. Cake. Repeat, everyone. Cake.
Learners	Cake. Cake.
Teacher	Right! If you eat cake, cake, cake and more cake, what's the result?
Learners	Stomacake!
Teacher	Right—stomacake! Stomach-ache. Repeat.
Learners	Stomach-ache.
Teacher	Perfect!

Unfortunately, nice remedial ideas do not exist for every spelling pronunciation problem.

The pronunciation of vocabulary items is normally taught first through listening, then imitation and repetition, and then feedback. For listening, it is important to first get the learners' attention: indicate with gestures that they should listen, not repeat. Then say the word or expression two or three times, naturally but clearly. For imitation and repetition, indicate with your hand that you want them to imitate and repeat the word or expression. Then get them to repeat it again several times, first in chorus, then some individual learners. For feedback, indicate whether their imitation is satisfactory or not, giving the model again if necessary.

If we take Extract 5 to the pronunciation stage, the whole sequence would continue like this:

Extract 5 (continued)

Teacher	That's right. He isn't American. Is he a foreigner in England?
Learner 3	No—he's English.
Teacher	Right. OK, now listen: /forenə/, /forenə/. Repeat, everyone.
Learners	Foreigner.
Teacher	Right. Omar, please.

In these examples, meaning is presented with real objects (realia) (Extract 1), examples (Extract 4), pictures (Extract 2), definition (Extract 5), demonstration (Extract 3), translation (Extract 6). Realia, pictures, and demonstration are especially useful for presenting the concrete vocabulary of beginners' and elementary courses. Examples are often useful at these levels also. Definitions as well as examples are especially useful for the more abstract vocabulary of upper elementary and intermediate courses. Translation, as we have already said, is best used as a last resort. It is also best, when possible, to elicit the translation from a learner, as in Extract 6. Involving learners actively can motivate them and help them remember the item.

You can also present meaning with mime and gesture, for example, 'driving a car', or 'swimming'. Using contrast, or antonyms is another technique, for example, 'This building is ugly. It isn't beautiful—it's ugly. Ugly.' The opposite of using *antonyms* is using equivalence, or *synonyms*, for example, 'They're having a chat—a conversation.' Presenting the meaning of vocabulary items, avoiding translation as much as possible, is an opportunity for creativity and ingenuity in teaching.

An important point to note about the extracts above is that the vocabulary is presented in a context, not as isolated words. An appropriate context helps learners begin to understand the use of the item as well as its basic meaning. The item is associated with a certain type of context or situation. 'Upset', for example, is associated with people's feelings or reactions to events.

Another important point to note about the extracts is that the teacher usually checks that the learners have understood. For example, in Extract 1 the teacher gets a learner to show his own wallet, and in Extract 4, the teacher gets the learners to give more examples of singers. Note also that in Extracts 1 and 5 the teacher checks whether any learners already know the item— 'She doesn't understand—she's a foreigner. A foreigner? No?' Remember, there may be learners who do already know the item. Giving them the opportunity to show that knowledge can be motivating for them and set a good example of active participation for the whole group. This is especially true with false beginner and intermediate learners.

Pronunciation and spelling

Obviously, learners must be able to recognize and produce the form of a new vocabulary item as well as understand its meaning and use. They must learn how the new item is pronounced, and how it is written. It is usually best to present new items orally first and in written form later, especially at lower levels (see Chapter 2). The main advantage to this procedure when dealing with new vocabulary is that you can avoid learners getting into the habit of using 'spelling pronunciation'. For example, in a lesson on health problems,

Learner 4	Foreigner.
Teacher	Good. Rebecca.
Learner 5	Foreigner.

In your oral models, try to present both the sounds and the stress of the items clearly, but keeping the pronunciation as natural as possible.

Spelling in English often seems quite unrelated to pronunciation, for example, in words like 'knight', 'castle', 'island', 'foreigner', and 'enough'. However, there are regular patterns in English spelling, and regular relationships between spelling and pronunciation. Where these exist, it can be useful to present the written forms of words earlier—for example, if learners are saying /kʌf/ instead of /kʌp/ for 'cup', and the spelling clarifies that it is /p/ not /f/. When you do write a new word or expression on the board, it is a good idea to say it aloud and get the learners to repeat it.

Teaching ideas

Here are three ideas to help your learners learn and revise vocabulary:

- Use a word-square to work on recognition of words. The task is for learners to find as many words as they can in the square, for example:

L	I	S	T	E	N
C	R	S	U	N	F
A	E	Q	P	U	L
T	A	B	L	E	O
P	L	R	A	W	O
O	D	A	Y	I	R

- Use a letter-bank to work on production of words. The task is for learners to write as many words as they can with the letters in a long word, for example:

WOLVERHAMPTON

Some of the words here are 'love', 'town', 'ham', 'mother', and 'wear'. There are at least another 25 words.

- Get learners to write key-words in columns to revise spelling-pronunciation relationships, for example:

Put the words in the box in the correct column according to the vowel sound:

said	eight	lie	see /iː/	day /ei/	line /ai/	pet /e/
mean	find	plate	_____	_____	_____	_____
pint	key	head	_____	_____	_____	_____
we	pen	rain	_____	_____	_____	_____

Grammar

Apart from the meaning, use in communication, pronunciation, and spelling of new words, learners need an idea of how they function in sentences. In Extracts 1 to 6 above, there were nouns ('knight', 'castle', 'singer', 'wallet', and 'foreigner'), a verb ('jump'), and an adjective ('upset'). An appropriate context of presentation usually makes this kind of grammatical information clear without any need for grammatical terminology, but problems may still arise.

With the word 'foreigner', used in Extract 5 above, some learners may say things like *'She's a foreigner student'. In that case you would need to clarify that 'foreigner' is a noun, and the adjective is 'foreign'. At other times you may need to point out that an item has more than one grammatical function, for example, 'farm' can be a noun, verb, or adjective. This kind of information is more appropriate for intermediate or advanced courses when learners can handle it without getting confused. The grammatical information you give learners should normally be only what they need and can assimilate at that moment. Try not to confuse them with information that is not relevant at their stage of learning English.

Question

What difficulties might your learners have with the following words?

wall, floor, ceiling	/wɔːl/ /flɔː/ /siːlɪŋ/
explain, play, agree	/ekspleɪn/ /pleɪ/ /əgriː/
actual, funny, short	/aektʃəl/ /fʌni/ /ʃɔːt/

Remember that presentation of new vocabulary items will not mean that learners have 'learnt' those items completely and forever. We really only know words and expressions when we have heard, read, said, or written them fairly frequently. This is true of our own language as well as of a foreign language. Most people are ignorant or uncertain about many words in their own language. If you want your learners to remember vocabulary and be able to use it in communication, you need to make sure it is used often. One way to do this is to get the learners, especially more advanced ones, to read as much as possible. But you usually need to practise vocabulary in class too.

Working on vocabulary

You can use a range of vocabulary in class warm-ups, and also in the lead-ins to the presentation of new items when establishing the context or situation. A well-planned coursebook also continually reactivates previously introduced vocabulary items, and may have specific vocabulary exercises. But usually you also need to organize practice activities to work on specific areas of vocabulary.

Teaching ideas

Here are some types of vocabulary practice activity:

- **Brainstorming**
  Get the learners to think of as many words as possible related to a specific topic, for example the topic of the lesson. This can be organized as a team competition. Each team lines up in front of the board, which is divided into sections, one for each team. The first person in each team goes to the board, writes a word in their section, and then goes to the back of the line. Then the second person goes to the board and writes a different word, and so on. Each team should write new words on the board as fast as they can until you say time is up. Then check to see which team has the most correct words.

- **Labelling**
  This is similar to brainstorming but with a chart or picture to aid the learners. It is especially suitable for topics like 'parts of the body' or 'things in the kitchen'. Again it can be handled as a team competition. Separate drawings or pictures can be put on the board or a wall for each team. Alternatively, the teams can take turns to label one picture, using different coloured chalk or markers.

- **Miming**
  Give a learner from one team a piece of paper with an activity written on it (for example, sail a boat, eat an ice-cream, fly a small plane). That learner has to mime the activity so that the other team members can guess it in a given time—for example, one minute. Then do the same with a learner from the next team. The winning team is the one that has guessed most activities when all the pieces of paper are finished.

- **Oral fill-in**
  Select or write an appropriate story. Leave out words that the learners
  should be able to guess from the context or with help from you miming.
  Then tell the story as if you could not think of some words and need the
  learners to help you, for example:

Teacher	One day I was at home sitting in an . . . er . . . er . . .
	[*Teacher mimes sitting in an armchair.*]
Learners	. . . armchair . . .
Teacher	Yes. I was reading the . . . er . . . [*Teacher mimes reading a*
	newspaper.]
Learners	. . . newspaper . . .
Teacher	Yes. In the newspaper I saw an . . . er . . . an . . .

- **Classification**
  Write words related to two or more topics mixed together on the board.
  Ask the learners to identify the topics and then to decide which words are
  associated with which topic. For example, you could mix words like 'tyre',
  'blender', 'boots', 'saucepan', 'goal', and 'brake'. These relate to three
  topics: cars ('tyre', 'brake'); cooking ('blender', 'saucepan'), and football
  ('boots', 'goal').

Remedial work

You need to become aware of your learners' typical vocabulary problems, try
to understand the causes, and plan remedial work when necessary. As with
all remedial work, it is best to start by helping the learners to notice what
they are saying wrong. Then you can get them to *self-* or *peer-correct*. A little
lively drilling can often help as well. Of course, you should not expect
learners to remember and use every one of the words and expressions that
occur in the coursebook or classes. Many words will at best be only in their
passive vocabulary. That means they may understand or recognize certain
words in context when they hear or read them, but they will not be able to
use them in their own speaking or writing. Words that are available for
learners to use in their own speaking and writing belong to their *active
vocabulary*.

Summary

In Chapter 4 we have considered the following points:

Vocabulary in language teaching and learning. Vocabulary is of enormous
importance in communication, but is sometimes neglected in English
language courses. Learning words and how to use them can be interesting
and satisfying, but it does involve complex knowledge. It also means helping
learners remember vocabulary. You have to consider how to reactivate

previously introduced vocabulary as well as what new vocabulary to introduce. New vocabulary may occur unexpectedly, and you have to be prepared to deal with it or openly confess when you need to refer to a dictionary.

Dealing with new vocabulary. It is generally necessary to know the meaning, communicative use, pronunciation, spelling, and grammar of words. It is usually best not to present meaning through translation first. Most vocabulary items can be presented clearly without translation, and other techniques involve the learners more and help them remember. You can use real objects, pictures, demonstration, examples, definition, mime, antonyms, and synonyms. It is also best to present vocabulary in context. Presentation of the oral form before the written form can help avoid 'spelling pronunciation', especially at beginner and elementary levels. Spending a little time on listening, imitation, and repetition of new words can also help with pronunciation. Work on spelling and spelling-pronunciation relationships can be done with games and competitions. Learners also need to know how words function grammatically in sentences. Presentation and initial practice of new vocabulary items is not enough. They need to be continually used by the learners.

Working on vocabulary. Some vocabulary can be kept active through classroom use of English, but specific practice activities are usually necessary too. These may include brainstorming topic vocabulary, miming and guessing words, completing an oral fill-in, and classifying scrambled words by topic.

Remedial work. Learners sometimes get mistaken ideas about certain words, and remedial work is necessary. Not all vocabulary needs to be kept active for use in speaking and writing. Some may be passive vocabulary that is understood but not produced.

Project

Organizing vocabulary activities

Purpose: to develop an ability to organize effective vocabulary practice.

Procedure:

1 Decide on one or more areas of vocabulary that the learners have already encountered and that you would like to reactivate and consolidate. You may look at a lesson in a coursebook for ideas.

2 Decide which of the following types of activity would be most suitable: labelling, miming, oral fill-in, classification (see the description of each on pages 67 and 68).

3 Develop the material and plan for the activity or activities.
4 If you are teaching, try the activity or activities out with your learners. If you are not yet teaching, leave the activity or activities for a day or two before examining the material again.
5 Reflect upon what changes might improve in the content and procedures for the activity or activities.

5 DEVELOPING SPOKEN COMMUNICATION SKILLS

Introduction

In this chapter we look at the nature of spoken communication. We compare communication outside and inside classrooms, and consider how to make the latter more like the former. We focus on how to develop listening comprehension skills, and then speaking skills. An important element in this is the use of English as the main classroom language (see Chapter 1), but specific listening and speaking activities are also necessary.

Communication

Periods of focusing on language form are important in foreign language learning, but developing the ability to really communicate in English is the main goal of an English language course. At the end of a course, the learners should be able to communicate effectively in English outside the classroom for study, work, or leisure.

Communication outside the classroom

How do we use language in communication outside the classroom? In our L1 we have conversations and carry out transactions, listen to the radio or television, read newspapers, magazines, and books, write notes or letters, and sometimes essays or longer texts. Some people regularly do some, or all, of these things in a second language, for example immigrants and foreign students. Many more use a foreign language, very often English, reading professional books and journals, attending courses or conferences, travelling abroad, and in social and professional contact with foreigners.

All of these communicative uses of language have certain features in common:

– We communicate because we want to or need to, not just to practise the language.
– Our attention is focused on *what* we are communicating (for example, information, ideas, opinions, feelings), not on *how* we are communicating (for example, the grammar of the language).
– The language is usually very varied in grammar and vocabulary, and a single structure or a few structures are not normally repeated over and over again.

We should try to create these features of natural communication in our classrooms.

Task

Look at the following text extracts and decide which might occur in normal communication situations, and which seem unlikely outside a classroom:

Extract 1

A Okay. Let's fill this in. What's your full name?
B Ana Maria Larios. That's L-A-R-I-O-S.
A Right. And your address and telephone?
B Thirty-five Avenida Reforma. I . . . er . . . haven't got a phone yet. In a week, I hope.
A I see. Well, let me know when you've got it.
B Yes, of course.

Extract 2

A What's your name?
B It's Oscar Moreno.
A What's your address?
B It's 100 Avenida Central.
A What's your telephone number?
B It's 403635.

Extract 3

Tom is taller than Mary, but Jack is shorter than her. Jack is older than Mary, but Tom is younger than her. Tom is very tall for his age. Jack is short, but he is strong. He is stronger than the other boys in his class. Mary is more intelligent than Jack or Tom. She always gets top marks in her class. She is also more artistic than her brothers. She can play the piano and sing. Jack and Tom are more athletic. Jack is in the school soccer team, and Tom is in the basketball team. They are a happy family. They do not fight now they are older and more mature.

Extract 4

Scientists have discovered that when chimpanzees have stomach pains, typically because of intestinal parasites, they look for a certain plant to eat, Lippea. It is common in the jungles where chimpanzees live, and it contains chemical substances effective against many parasites. Lippea is not the only natural medicine in the chimpanzees' cabinet. They may actually use up to thirty different plants—for different problems. Interestingly, the local people make use of many of the same plants for medical purposes. It is almost certain that chimpanzees discovered these herbal remedies before humans.

In Extracts 1 and 2, real personal information is communicated. But the repetition of the same type of question and answer in Extract 2 is very unnatural. In contrast, Extract 1 is more naturally unpredictable, and the language is that of an authentic conversation. In Extract 3, Jack, Mary, and Tom seem to be invented characters of no real interest to a reader, and the repetition of comparatives is unnatural. In contrast, Extract 4 has varied language and contains information of wide general interest: it might, for example, be taken from a magazine article.

Extracts 2 and 3 are 'teaching texts', designed to consolidate specific language forms. Extracts 1 and 4 are from the world of 'real communication situations' where people have job interviews and read magazines. All four extracts could be used for listening or reading comprehension in an English language course. But Extracts 1 and 4 would prepare the learners much better for the use of English in real communication situations outside the classroom than Extracts 2 and 3.

Communication is not just a matter of information and language. It also involves purpose and attitude. Our attention is focused on the ideas communicated, not on the language used. It is unlikely that anyone except a language student would either need or want to read a text like Extract 3. In contrast, Extract 4 would be likely to attract many readers, who might even mention the topic to relatives, friends or colleagues.

Communication in the classroom

It is one thing to want communicative interactions like Extracts 1 and 4 in your classroom, and quite another thing to make them happen. How can you get something like them in the limited and 'special' context of the classroom? Well, you can:

– Establish English as the main classroom language—without that, the development of oral communication skills will be very restricted.
– Try to use interesting topics and stimulating activities, which take the learners' minds off the language, at least a little.
– Support and encourage learners in their efforts to communicate their ideas instead of trying to control what they say and interrupting them to correct their language mistakes.

The classroom is certainly a very specific context for communication. There are four walls with a board on one of them. The same teacher and learners meet class after class, and visitors are usually very rare. And the class takes place at the same time on the same days.

If you want real communication, you will need to exploit:

– events and changes in the classroom (for example, the weather, the learners' clothes, their health and mood, and pictures and *realia* you and the learners bring to the class)
– events in the world outside (for example, a circus in town, a national sports victory, the learners' families, new films)
– potentially interesting listening and reading texts, like Extract 4
– potentially useful or amusing *role-plays* and *simulations*.

Without your imaginative use of these and other resources, the limitations of the classroom can severely restrict communication.

The four skills

In language teaching, communication is usually divided into four main skills: listening, speaking, reading, and writing. Listening and reading are receptive skills, and speaking and writing are productive skills. There was a time when the terms 'passive' and 'active' were often used instead of 'receptive' and 'productive'. But it is now generally agreed that effective listening and reading require as much attention and mental activity as speaking and writing.

Two common misconceptions are that the productive skills are more 'communicative' than the receptive skills, and also that they are the basis of the learning process itself. To some extent these misconceptions are understandable. Everyone likes quick, tangible results, for example, learners producing lots of sentences in English. But children begin to learn their mother tongue by listening before they speak, and the same is true of immigrants or foreign residents learning a second language. Both children and learners of a second, or foreign, language have wide, varied exposure, which helps them learn the language and develop communication skills.

Rather than emphasizing the productive skills at the expense of the receptive skills, it is better to exploit the natural relationships between them, for example, the skills of listening and speaking are combined in conversation. Outside the classroom, we continually integrate the skills or switch from one to another. It is important to replicate this natural integration of skills in the classroom as much as possible. Apart from reflecting the natural use of language, it offers different opportunities for different types of learners, for example, the extroverts who like to speak a lot, the introverts who prefer to listen or read, and the analytically or visually oriented learners who like to see how words are written and sentences constructed.

Listening

Some learners say 'I understand everything but I can't speak'. This may be the case when people speak slowly and carefully to them, realizing that they do not know much English. But it is usually very different when they are listening to English programmes on the radio, or watching English television or films, or trying to take part in conversations dominated by native speakers. Listening is as difficult as any of the other skills. In fact, learners often find it hard to understand coursebook cassettes especially designed for them. Unlike reading texts, the speed and clarity of spoken texts are often completely outside the listener's control. If you do not understand the words while they are still 'in the air', it is usually too late. Of course, this is not always so. In a conversation you can ask the other person to speak more slowly, or repeat or explain something. In fact, these are very useful strategies for learners to acquire and use in conversation and similar situations. Table 5.1 classifies listening texts in terms of listener control.

Type	Situation
No listener control	Public announcement
↓	Radio, television, cinema, theatre
	Overheard conversation
	Public lecture
	Class or seminar
	Interview
↑	Telephone conversation
Some listener control	Face-to-face conversation

Table 5.1: Degrees of listener control in relation to listening texts

Remember, you are giving the learners listening practice when using English as the main classroom language (class or seminar) and in pair and groupwork (face-to-face conversation). Also, these are listening situations where the learners do have some control and can use the strategies mentioned above. Encourage them to ask for things to be repeated or explained if necessary, and teach them appropriate expressions, for example, 'Could you repeat that, please?' and 'I'm sorry. I didn't understand that.'

In natural listening situations, like those in Table 5.1, we appear to use specific listening strategies:

– We usually start listening with certain expectations. For example, at an airport we expect to hear about flight numbers, gate numbers, delays, and cancellations. And when watching a science-fiction film we expect to hear about spacecraft and extraterrestrials.

– As we listen, we try to confirm or identify the precise topic, and each change of topic. This activates ideas we already have about that topic, which helps us make sense of what we then hear. The word 'dolphins' probably brings a lot into your mind. 'Dolines' probably brings nothing into your mind, although it is a real English word.

– We try to recognize as many words and phrases as possible. The flow of speech which sounds something like 'WATchupriFER?' probably consists of the words 'What do you prefer?' But even native speakers with perfect hearing, in conditions where there is no problem of low volume, rapid speech, or background noise, seldom hear and recognize every single word addressed to them. And non-native speakers, especially in poor conditions, may miss many words and phrases.

– We try to create a coherent text in our mind from what we hear, using what we know about the topic on the one hand and about the English language on the other:

> Dolphins protect . . . selves . . . sharks . . . ramming . . . the side, where their liver is. Dolphins . . . manoeuvre faster and better . . . water than sharks, . . . no real danger . . .

might be interpreted as:

> Dolphins protect themselves from sharks by ramming them in the side, where their liver is. Dolphins can manoeuvre faster and better in the water than sharks, so there's no real danger for them.

– We respond to what we understand while and after we listen to it. For example, we may begin to run if we hear we are in danger of missing our flight. Or we may think things like 'That's interesting' or 'I don't agree with that' when listening to a lecture.

Classroom listening

As we have emphasized, your greetings, questions, instructions, explanations, anecdotes and so on, are probably the most natural and generally effective listening comprehension practice you can provide in the classroom. When you use English consistently in this way, you are giving the learners meaningful, authentic listening practice. It has a clear purpose, it is focused on the message rather than on the language, and it can be quite varied. You can expand the range of English you use as the course progresses and encourage your learners to use it as much as possible. When the learners also use English for most classroom purposes, both with the teacher and their peers, the listening practice time is increased enormously. Pair and groupwork can also provide extensive listening as well as speaking practice. But classroom listening of these kinds is rather restricted. Amongst other things, it is limited to the speech of the teacher and the learners. So it is very useful to bring into the classroom recorded speech in situations from the world outside, and with a variety of voices and accents.

Recorded texts

Recorded texts may include all the types of listening referred to in the table. Your coursebook cassette will probably be the source of most, or even all, of these. If it is of good quality, at least some of the texts will be authentic (for example, extracts from real radio programmes). Good listening texts should contain interesting information or present situations the learners may really meet outside the classroom. However, the text itself is only one element in a listening activity. Equally important is how you approach it and the activities you use with it. You can make coursebook or other listening practice more realistic and interesting by following specific stages and using specific techniques. The stages generally recommended are:

Pre-listening

This stage is to prepare the learners for what they are going to hear, just as we are usually prepared in real life (for example, we usually have expectations about the topic, and even the language). You should not just tell the learners to listen and then start the cassette.

While-listening

This stage is to help the learners understand the text. You should not expect them to try to understand every word. For example, you may ask them to listen for three pieces of information the first time they hear the recording, and to tell you about the attitude of the speakers after the second time they have heard it. In general, you should help your learners understand rather than testing their understanding the whole time.

Post-listening

This stage is to help the learners connect what they have heard with their own ideas and experience, just as we often do in real life. It also allows you to move easily from listening to another language skill. For example, the learners may practise speaking by role-playing interviews similar to one they have heard.

Teaching ideas

Among the many possible pre-, while-, and post-listening activities are:

- **Pre-listening:**
  Discuss a relevant picture
  Discuss relevant experiences
  Associate ideas with the topic
  Associate vocabulary with the topic
  Predict information about the topic
  Write questions about the topic

- **While-listening:**
  Identify the exact topic, or an aspect of it
  Note two to four pieces of information
  Answer questions
  Complete sentences
  Complete a table, map, or picture

- **Post-listening:**
  Give opinions
  Relate similar experiences
  Role-play a similar interaction
  Write a brief report
  Write a similar text
  Debate the topic

There is some controversy about whether a recording should be played over and over again in the while-listening stage. Some teachers insist that this is unnatural and unlike most real-life listening situations, where you get only one opportunity to understand. But most teachers think that classroom listening practice can be different from real-life listening and still be useful preparation for it.

It is best to give very simple tasks the first time the learners hear a recording, and increasingly difficult ones the second or third times. This is much better than giving them a single, complex task from the start and playing the text over and over again, hoping the learners will recover from their initial shock, and confusion, and eventually complete most of the task.

One way of gradually getting even elementary learners to understand most of a text the first time they hear it, is to use parallel texts. For example, you may have a tourist excursion announcement on your coursebook cassette. Record two or three modified versions of it, for example, with different destinations, departure times, and lunch arrangements, using different teachers to record each version if possible. After an appropriate pre-listening activity, play the original version several times until the learners have grasped all the important information. Then play the second version, challenging the learners to catch most of the information the first time they hear it. They should understand it all after two hearings at most. With the third and fourth versions, which can be used in later lessons, they should understand almost everything the first time, just as if they were really hearing an announcement at a tourist hotel.

This process is like the development of the listening skill in real life. Babies hear their mothers use the same words and phrases over and over again, regular travellers hear similar announcements, and regular television news watchers hear similar news formats night after night. Familiarity with a certain kind of listening text or context can aid comprehension significantly.

Task

Look at the coursebook listening exercise on page 80.

The text is fairly typical of an airport announcement. But listening to an airport announcement in the classroom is not a natural listening experience. The communicative purpose is not clear. Why would a traveller want to know *all* the information? Also, although the text is short, it is full of information. To answer all the questions, it is necessary to understand almost every word. But you could exploit this text, and the illustration, to provide effective listening practice.

Consider how you would organize part of a lesson using the above material. Think in terms of the three stages—pre-listening, while-listening, and post-listening. Think carefully about the purpose of your pre-listening activity. Make your first while-listening activity easy. Connect the post-listening activity with real life.

Listening

You are at an international airport. Listen to the announcements and answer the questions.

BRITISH AIRWAYS FLIGHT 269	AEROMEXICO FLIGHT 129	AMERICAN AIRLINES FLIGHT 409
FROM LONDON	TO CANCÚN	TO HOUSTON AND LIMA
	BOARDING GATE 6	DELAYED TO 1600 HOURS

1 Which flight is arriving?
2 Which flight is going to leave?
3 What is the gate number for that flight?
4 Which flight is going to leave late?
5 What is the new time for that flight?

Listening text:
Your attention please for the following announcements. British Airways flight 269 from London is now arriving . . . Passengers for Aeromexico flight 129 to Cancún please proceed to Gate 6, where this flight is now boarding . . . American Airlines regrets the delay of its flight 409 to Houston with final destination Lima. This flight will now depart at sixteen hundred hours.

The ideas that follow may be quite different from what you planned, but your ideas should be based on the same principles. You could begin establishing the context by asking questions about the illustration. You could also ask who has flown, or accompanied relatives or friends to the airport, and allow learners to talk a little about their experiences. Then ask what kind of things they would expect to hear in an airport announcement. This might produce some essential vocabulary, for example, 'flight', 'gate', 'delay', 'board', and 'depart'. It does not matter if some of the learners' responses are in their native language, or if they ask 'How do you say _____ in English?'

Then you could substitute the coursebook task with a more realistic and active one. Tell a third of the class that they are going to Houston or Lima, another third that they are meeting a friend from London, and the final third that they are going to Cancún. You need to give them very clear instructions, for example:

Teacher	OK, so who's going to Houston? Raise your hands. Good. And Lima. OK. And who's meeting a friend from London? OK. And who's going to Cancún? OK—lucky people! Right, now listen carefully. When you hear your flight, stand up. If the flight is late, say 'Oh, no!' and sit down again. If it is on time, say 'Good!' and stay standing.

Check that they have understood:

Teacher	When you hear your flight, you . . .
Learners	. . . stand up.
Teacher	If the flight is late . . .
Learners	. . . say 'Oh, no!' and sit down.
Teacher	If the flight is on time . . .
Learners	. . . say 'Good!' and stay standing.

After you have played the cassette once, check with several learners what the situation is with their flight. After that, play the cassette again, and get the groups to note down just the information related to their own flight. Finally, play the cassette for a third time, and get everyone to answer all the questions in the book. After the while-listening activities, you could use the topic or situation for further skills practice. For example, you could ask some learners to relate an experience they have had waiting for someone at an airport, or you could get groups to write similar announcements and then read them out.

This example gives a useful general procedure for listening comprehension work, but not all practice will be just like it. Among other things, the activities you use should depend on the difficulty of the text and the level of the learners. Listening to songs, for example, may involve quite different procedures from those suggested here (see Chapter 10, pages 163–5).

Speaking

Speaking comes naturally to humans, but it is not as simple as it seems. For a start:

– Many people do not like speaking in front of large groups of people. This is especially true in a foreign language, because we may worry about producing utterances with many errors or oddities in them.
– Recognizable pronunciation is necessary for speech to be intelligible. It is sometimes hard to understand people with a strong regional accent in our own language, and it is hard to interpret a non-native speaker's 'Ease . . . eat . . . tree . . . jet?' as 'Is it three yet?'
– Like listening, speaking takes place in 'real time', and speakers do not usually have time to construct their utterances carefully. In conversation, the commonest kind of speaking, we have to do many things all together: understand what the other person is saying, say what we want to when we get the chance to speak, be prepared for unexpected changes of topic, and think of something to say when there is a long pause.

There are some clear implications here for teaching:

– Try to create a relaxed atmosphere in your classes so that most learners are not frightened of speaking in front of the rest of the class. And do as many speaking activities as possible in pairs and groups, so that the learners can speak English without the rest of the class listening.
– Expose the learners as much as possible to naturally pronounced speech, and also integrate some pronunciation work into your lessons. They will not learn to pronounce intelligibly, or to develop speaking skills in general, if they do not hear enough natural speech.
– Accustom the learners to combining listening and speaking in real time, in natural interaction. Perhaps the most important opportunity for this is in the general use of English in the classroom.

Classroom speaking

Like listening ability, speaking ability should partly be the natural result of using English as the main means of communication in the classroom. But speaking will probably develop more slowly than listening. You can help learners understand what you say in English by simplifying your speech and using gesture or mime. You cannot so easily get them to express themselves in English, but, when they do, always show you are pleased even if what they say is far from perfect.

Try to take every opportunity in class to get the learners to use language that has been introduced previously. Ask them questions, or ask them to tell you about something. For example, if you are going to use pictures of two popular seaside resorts to present and practise comparison with adjectives, you could develop a conversation like this:

Teacher	Who's visited this place? Ana? Good. Where is it?
Learner 1	Veracruz.
Teacher	That's right. When did you go there?
Learner 1	The last year.
Teacher	Ah—last year. Tell us about your visit.
Learner 1	I was . . . I went with my family. We went four days.
Teacher	Very nice. Ask Ana about her holiday—what she did, the discos, the boys . . .
Learner 2	What you did—What did you do in Veracruz?

The conversational use of English can also be achieved with learners working in pairs or groups. For example, if you are going to use a photograph of Madonna to present and practise the Present Perfect—countries where she has given concerts, records she has sold, films she has made—you could first exploit the topic like this:

Teacher	Do you recognize her?
Learner 1	Er . . . Madonna?
Teacher	Right. What do you know about her?
Learner 2	She's American. She . . .
Teacher	. . . Good. You know a lot. Now, in groups of three exchange your opinions of Madonna as a singer, and Madonna as a person.

If you want the learners to be able to converse in English, you need to make the classroom a conversational place. If the learners do not talk naturally during the course of each lesson, it is hardly surprising when they can still hardly speak at all after hundreds of hours and several years of English classes.

Speaking activities

We have already considered a range of oral practice activities, from controlled accuracy work to fairly free fluency work (see Chapter 3). All the activities in this progression from accuracy to fluency can contribute to the development of speaking skills. Even non-communicative oral practice can help develop pronunciation and the fairly automatic production of grammatical sequences of words. But it is the types of activity that develop the ability to participate effectively in interactions outside the classroom that are most relevant in this chapter.

Among the speaking activities described in Chapter 3 were script-based role-plays or simulations, script-based conversations, and form-based interviews or surveys (see pages 48–50). These activities were included there because the examples given were designed to elicit repetition of specific grammatical-functional items. Although they are examples of activities designed to encourage learners to communicate as naturally as possible, teachers and learners would be aware that recently presented language was being practised. Attention would almost inevitably be focused to a considerable extent on the new language forms.

In natural communication, attention is not usually focused on the language used, but on the messages it conveys. These messages are only partially predictable, for the topic may change quite suddenly. The language is also only partially predictable. In natural listening–speaking situations the listeners must be able to handle such shifts of topic and unpredictable language in listening, and then they must be able to improvise their responses.

The feasibility of providing opportunities for learners to speak naturally in class will depend to a large extent on the type of learners and course you are teaching. With beginners and with very large groups, the possibilities may be quite limited. In such circumstances, you may have to be satisfied with incidental classroom speaking, and some carefully planned and organized fluency practice activities like those mentioned above. However, you can repeat some of these same activities later in a course without such extensive preparation, or following the careful steps suggested in Chapter 3. The learners will then have to work partly from their memory of the original activity, and partly improvise. They will no longer be using language that has just been presented. In fact, they will have to function almost as if they were using English in communication outside the classroom. Here is an example:

Teacher	Do you remember the consultation with a doctor? We did it last month.
Learner 1	Yes . . .
Learner 2	More or less . . .
Teacher	More or less—right, Victor! What were some of the patients' problems?
Learner 3	Headache, stomach-ache, backache, earache.
Teacher	Right—lots of aches! What else?
Learner 4	Insomnia, nausea.
Teacher	Right. Now, in pairs, imagine you're in a doctor's surgery. One of you is the doctor and the other is the patient.

It is important in this kind of activity to monitor as many pairs as possible, noting how well they might manage in a real consultation. You should also note language problems that will need attention later. The pairwork can be followed by a few pairs acting out a consultation in front of the class.

Some of these activities also allow the more fluent learners to go beyond the original script. For example, a role-play consisting of a conversation at a party can go beyond the names, occupations, and current activities of the model script. You can tell the learners to extend the conversation if they can, and talk about things such as likes and dislikes, and places they have visited. In fact, you could have a 'party', a 'wedding' or a 'cruise' once a month, and encourage all the learners to go beyond the original script.

These kinds of activity can be used even with beginners, especially highly motivated ones. But they will probably work best in upper elementary, intermediate, or advanced groups, and in smaller groups of learners. Below there are some other activities you can use with this kind of group.

Teaching ideas

- **Unscripted role-plays**
  These differ from scripted role-plays or simulations because the learners have only a description of a situation and no model script, for example:

  > The living room of a house at one o'clock in the morning. The parents have been waiting up. The 14-year-old son/daughter has just arrived home.

  They may also have a card for each role, for example:

Mother	you are furious; you phoned your son/daughter's best friends, Adam and Alice. Your son/daughter was not with either.

Father	you are a bit angry, but you are tired and would prefer to go to bed and talk tomorrow.

Son/Daughter	start by lying that you were studying at Adam's house; then that you were at a party at Alice's house; finally, tell the truth—you went to a disco.

  Get the learners to improvise the discussion in groups of three—Mother, Father, and Son/Daughter. If they have role cards, they should not look at one anothers' cards. When the groups have finished their improvisations, get one or more of them to act out their role-play in front of the class.

- **Problem-solving/decision-taking activities**
  Describe a problem to the learners, or give them a written description, for example:

You see a fellow worker in your office steal a portable computer; you know he/she is the single parent of two young children and has financial problems.

Get the learners, in groups of three to five, to decide what the best course of action is.

- **Discussions and debates**
  Organize an informal discussion or a formal debate on a topic of interest to the learners. Get them to propose or select the topic. It is often best to decide on the topic the lesson before the actual discussion or debate.

- **Group projects**
  Get groups of three to five learners to prepare posters for the cause of their choice, for example, save the rainforest, support a street children's home, or support AIDS research. If you hear anyone speaking in their L1 as they work on the project the group loses a point. There is an exhibition of the posters, and all the learners vote for the best one (15 points), the second best (10 points) and the third best (5 points). Deduct any points for speaking the L1 during the project work. The group with the most points wins.

- **Warm-ups and fillers**
  There are many other very simple but effective speaking activities, especially for intermediate or small groups. Some are particularly good as warm-ups at the beginning of lessons, or fillers at the end. For example, simply say 'What a great holiday that was!', and then sit down and wait for questions. If nobody asks a question, you can write cues on the board, for example, 'When . . .?', 'Where . . .?', 'Who with . . .?', 'How long . . .?' After you have answered a good number of questions, put the learners into groups and invite one person in each group to say 'What a great holiday that was!' Other topics can be handled in the same way, for example, 'What a terrible night that was!', 'What an interesting person she is!', 'What a beautiful place it is!', or 'What an exciting experience that was!'

Summary

In Chapter 5 we have considered the following points:

Communication. Outside the classroom we communicate because we really want or need to, focusing on information and ideas, not the language, and using varied grammar and vocabulary. In order to promote real communicative ability, establish English as the classroom language, use interesting topics and stimulating activities, and support and encourage the learners in every effort they make to communicate. Communication skills can be divided into listening, speaking, reading, and writing, but these are often combined. The receptive skills (listening, reading) are as important and as complex as the productive skills (speaking, writing).

Listening. Some people say listening is much easier than speaking, but understanding normal conversation, the radio, or public announcements is hard for most people. What we hear is usually outside our control and often unclear. Our knowledge of situations and topics helps us make sense of it. Using English in the classroom as much as possible is fundamental in developing listening comprehension, but needs to be supplemented with recorded texts from varied situations outside the classroom. Listening comprehension is best taught in three stages: pre-, while-, and post-listening. The first stage prepares learners, the second develops and checks comprehension, and the third relates what they heard to their own experience.

Speaking. Conversation is difficult for many learners because it takes place in 'real time' and involves various skills. Public speaking inhibits people. While learning to speak our L1 or a foreign language, we inevitably make mistakes. For all these reasons, you should create a relaxed atmosphere, accustom the learners to listening and speaking in natural interaction, organize pair and groupwork, and avoid any obsession with accuracy. Encourage incidental classroom speaking, giving learners the expressions they need, and exploit every opportunity for 'conversation'. Some fluency practice activities presented in Chapter 3 can be repeated and developed without any specific language focus. Many other speaking activities have essentially communicative, not linguistic objectives. These include unscripted role-plays or simulations, problem-solving/decision-taking activities, discussions and debates, and group projects.

Project

Preparing an unscripted role-play or simulation

Purpose: To develop the ability to promote learners' speaking skills.

Procedure:

1 Study the example of an unscripted role-play on pages 85–6.
2 Think of an idea that you predict would appeal to your learners or the learners you might teach.
3 Prepare a clear description of the situation and role cards. Also plan the procedures you would follow in organizing the activity in class.
4 If you can use the activity in class, reflect afterwards on how it went, and what changes you would make if you used it again. If you are not yet teaching, leave the material for a week, then examine it again.

6 DEVELOPING WRITTEN COMMUNICATION SKILLS

Introduction

In this chapter we look at written language and show how it is different from spoken language. We focus on ways of developing reading comprehension skills, and then writing skills. Finally, we consider how the different skills of listening, speaking, reading, and writing can often be combined in foreign language classes just as they are in communication outside the classroom.

Spoken and written language

In speaking, we tend to leave out elements when they are obvious from the context, for example:

A Working?
B No, just writing a letter.

instead of:

A Are you working?
B No, I am not working. I am just writing a letter.

If we did not leave out elements like this, spoken communication would include a great number of unnecessary words and would take up an enormous amount of time.

In contrast, the written language is usually more grammatically complete. The main reason for this is that, unlike listeners, readers do not have tone of voice, facial expression, and gestures, or a real situational context to help them understand messages. A written text has to create context and make the references and connections of the messages clear through the language itself. This requires more grammatically complete and often longer sentences, and also a greater range of vocabulary and the use of grammatical structures that rarely occur in speech. But the fact that readers and writers can take their own time compensates for this greater complexity. Writers can plan, and then edit and correct early drafts of a text, and readers can reread passages that they do not understand at first.

Reading comprehension

Reading comprehension has much in common with listening comprehension, but also some differences. As is often the case in listening, we usually start reading with certain expectations: for example, in a newspaper we expect news, and on certain pages we expect financial news, entertainment news, or sports news. As we read, we try to confirm or identify the precise topic, and each change of topic. This activates the ideas we have stored in our mind related to that topic. And that helps us to make sense of what we then read. On the basis of our expectations, our previous ideas about the topic, and our knowledge of the language and of texts written in the language, to some extent we predict what will come next. When you have read:

England's greatest writer was born in 1564. His name . . .

you can probably predict that the verb that comes next will be 'was', and the name after that will be 'William Shakespeare'.

Fluent readers generally move from meaningful segment to meaningful segment in a text. They do not usually read:

England's—greatest—writer—was—born—in—1564.—His—name—was—William—Shakespeare.

nor:

England's greatest—writer was—born in—1564. His name—was William—Shakespeare.

but:

England's greatest writer—was born in 1564.—His name was—William Shakespeare.

We respond to what we read while and after reading: we may frown or smile, or even cry. Or we may think things like 'That's interesting', or 'Yes, I've heard about that before', or even 'I can't understand much of this'.

Figure 6.1 shows the way in which fluent reading comprehension probably functions.

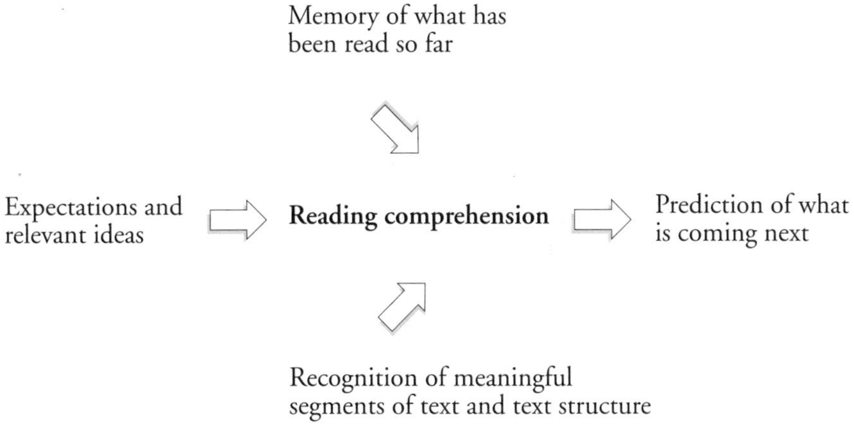

Memory of what has
been read so far

Expectations and   **Reading comprehension**   Prediction of what
relevant ideas   is coming next

Recognition of meaningful
segments of text and text structure

Figure 6.1: A model of reading comprehension

One important difference between reading and listening is that the text in reading is usually clearly, completely, and permanently on the page in front of us, while in listening the text is ephemeral and often not clear or complete. This permanence of reading texts has positive and negative sides, especially for non-native readers. On the positive side, people can read at their own pace, and reread things they do not understand immediately. On the negative side, some people read very slowly, word by word, even in their L1. Many more people do this in a foreign language. In fact, they often laboriously translate the text word by word. Reading comprehension in a foreign language is not translation, though translation may occasionally be useful. And it is not reading aloud. Reading comprehension work should normally deal with direct comprehension in silent reading. In other words, it should aim to develop the skills competent readers use in their L1.

Ways of reading

We often read in distinctly different ways for different purposes. Sometimes we do preliminary or exploratory reading rather than reading whole texts thoroughly. This kind of reading can be divided into two types, *scanning* and *skimming*. When scanning a text, you look quickly through it to find some specific information, for example, looking through a telephone directory for a specific number, a sports article for the result of a specific soccer game, or a textbook for the mention of a specific topic. When skimming, you look quickly through a text just to get a general idea of what it is about, in other words, the *gist*.

When we read whole texts we may also read in different ways at different times, depending, for example, on whether we are reading an easy text for pleasure or a difficult text for study or work. When reading a novel, for example, you may hardly be aware of the words on the page. The novel simply 'comes to life' in your head. Even with study or professional reading you may also read easily through a text if the text and content is simple or you are already familiar with the subject. But even in our L1 we sometimes have to work hard to understand a text. For example, articles or books on innovative or complex areas of science or technology may make us painfully aware of how we are struggling to attach intelligible ideas to the words on the page. Obviously, this happens more often in a foreign language.

In many English language courses, reading comprehension work consists only of scanning, skimming, and 'easy reading'. But you should not forget that professional people need to be able to deal with more complex texts as well. For example, doctors, engineers, or chemists need to be able to understand new, often revolutionary and complex, concepts and procedures very clearly indeed.

Reading activities

As we have said, reading has much in common with listening, and many aspects of the teaching of reading comprehension are similar to the teaching of listening comprehension. For example, the selection of texts is just as important. They should as far as possible be what the learners might really want or need to read. Many coursebooks nowadays contain potentially interesting reading texts, like the one about chimpanzee medicine on page 73. But you still need to be prepared to find alternatives to texts which are of little interest and are really trying to give practice in grammar not reading comprehension, like the one about Mary, Tom, and Jack on pages 72–3. If necessary, it is relatively easy to substitute or supplement the reading material in your coursebook with authentic material from magazines, newspapers, holiday brochures, and books. You may need to simplify such material for lower level classes, and you will need to design suitable activities and exercises. The text is only one element in a reading activity.

As in listening comprehension practice, three stages are generally recommended to make reading more realistic and interesting:

Pre-reading

This stage is to prepare the learners for what they are going to read, just as we are usually prepared in real life.

While-reading

This stage is to help the learners understand the text. They may first do an easy scanning or skimming task, and then a task requiring more thorough comprehension. As with listening, you should help your learners understand the text rather than just testing their comprehension the whole time.

Post-reading

This stage is to help the learners to connect what they have read with their own ideas and experience, just as we often do in real life, and perhaps to move fluently from reading to another classroom activity.

Teaching ideas

Pre-reading:
Guess the topic of the text from the headings, illustrations, etc.
Brainstorm around a topic word on the board, for example, 'sharks'.
Predict what the text will say.
Write questions that may be answered by the text.

While-reading:
Scan for two to four items of information.
Skim for the general idea.
Answer questions.
Complete sentences.
Complete a table, map, or picture.
Ask each other questions.

Post-reading:
Discuss what was interesting or new in the text.
Discuss or debate the topic of the text if it is controversial.
Do tasks on the language or structure of the text.
Summarize the text, either orally or in writing.

Look at the coursebook material opposite.

Your first reaction to this material might be that it would not interest many learners. If you are convinced that is the case, it may be best not to use it. But if you think a picture of Stonehenge would be recognized by some learners, and they might also know something about their own country's prehistory, you may be able to exploit the material quite well. You then need to think about pre-, while-, and post-reading activities.

Read the following text and then answer the questions.

The Beaker People were early inhabitants of Britain. They arrived from Spain in about 2000 BC. A beaker is a type of cup, and the Beaker People got their name because they buried ceramic beakers with their dead. They probably used the beakers for an alcoholic drink which they thought had magical properties.

The Beaker people introduced metal to Britain—bronze. They were warriors, and with metal axes and knives, they soon conquered the other inhabitants of Britain, who still used stone weapons.

We do not know what their clothes were like, but they wore gold ornaments, which they imported from Ireland. The chiefs had large wooden houses, but the ordinary people lived in very simple huts. They did not build permanent villages or towns, but periodically moved from place to place with their animals. They usually inhabited the valleys, but they buried their chiefs on hills and high places, in large tombs called 'barrows'.

As well as barrows, they built many of the most impressive prehistoric monuments in the south of England. They erected the gigantic circles of stones at Avebury and Stonehenge. These monuments almost certainly had a religious significance, but we do not know today exactly what the Beaker People used them for.

1 The Beaker People were originally from: (a) Britain (b) Ireland (c) Spain
2 Their name comes from: (a) an alcoholic drink (b) a kind of cup (c) magic
3 They were very: (a) passive (b) dynamic (c) primitive
4 They were successful because they used (a) stone (b) gold (c) bronze
5 They lived in (a) temporary settlements (b) towns on hills (c) large tombs
6 Their monuments are (a) not known now (b) made of large stones (c) all in one place

The coursebook material does not include any pre-reading activities. A large, dramatic picture or poster of Stonehenge would be an excellent aid. You could ask questions like:

Does anyone recognize this?
What do you think it is?
Where do you think it is?
How old do you think it is?
What do you think it was used for?
Is there anything like it in our country?

You could then discuss the Stone Age, the Bronze Age, and the Iron Age a little. That could produce some useful vocabulary.

The coursebook while-reading activity seems satisfactory, but you might like to add a preliminary scanning task, for example:

In 30 seconds, find the definitions in the text of 'beaker' and 'barrow'.

It is good to give time limits for skimming and scanning tasks so that the learners do not convert them into thorough reading tasks. As a post-reading activity, you could discuss pre-historic monuments learners have visited.

Exercises that require the learners to identify *cognates* and guess the meaning of unknown words from context are common in some syllabuses and materials. These can be useful strategies for serious reading in a foreign language, and certainly for motivating learners in the early stages. But they should not be emphasized too much, as the learners will get the impression that it is possible to read efficiently and reliably with very little knowledge of the language. Some words are false cognates (for example, 'lecture' in English—a spoken academic presentation—is not the equivalent of 'lectura' in Spanish, which means 'reading'). And guesses may be incorrect. Nothing can fully compensate for an adequate knowledge of the language.

Readers do not necessarily need good listening, speaking, and writing skills. But they do need to be able to recognize the meaning and function of most of the language elements in the texts they read. A reader who does not automatically understand the function of 'however', 'unless', 'as well as', 'due to', and 'hardly ever', as well as most of the nouns and verbs, cannot be relied upon to interpret a professional text accurately. This is especially true when the text contains innovative or complex ideas. Of course, the knowledge of the language necessary for reliable and efficient serious reading can probably be acquired to a large extent simply through reading extensively. At first it may be rather laborious and the comprehension rather unreliable, but both language knowledge and reading skills seem to develop with extensive reading.

Reading outside the classroom

It is sometimes hard to get learners to read more than the short texts you use in class. But reading is something that they can do at home, and you should encourage this as much as possible. For example, simplified readers, available from most major ELT publishers, are very useful at lower levels. If your school cannot afford to build up a library of readers, you could ask if the learners themselves are prepared to buy a different book each and build up a class library that way. At higher levels you can bring copies of articles you have selected from magazines, and let learners choose one to read at home. This might encourage them to read English language magazines by themselves. Extensive reading is an excellent way to extend vocabulary and consolidate grammar, as well as to develop a general communicative command of the language.

Writing

Writing is probably the linguistic skill that is least used by most people in their native language. Even in the most 'advanced' societies a significant percentage of the adult population writes with difficulty. Good writing skills usually develop from extensive reading, some specific training, and a good deal of practice.

Writing involves the following basic skills:

– handwriting or typing
– spelling
– constructing grammatical sentences
– punctuating.

Those learners whose language does not use the Roman alphabet may have to spend a considerable amount of time in getting a good command of the alphabet, spelling, and punctuation. A lot of this work may be done through reading activities—for example, word, phrase, and sentence recognition—as well as writing. You can organize some of the necessary practice as games and competitions.

At higher levels, writing involves cognitive skills such as:

– gathering information and ideas relevant to the topic, and discarding what is not relevant
– organizing the information and ideas into a logical sequence
– structuring the sequence into sections and paragraphs
– expressing the information and ideas in a written draft
– editing the draft and writing out a final text.

These composing skills are necessary for all formal writing, such as formal letters, academic assignments or articles, and business reports. They are not so necessary in the writing of informal letters. We may write the latter if as we were speaking, putting ideas down on paper as they come to us, often adding a postscript containing something we forgot when we were writing the main part of the letter.

Writing activities

Writing in an English language course may be handled in different ways for different purposes. The aim of the commonest type of writing practice is to consolidate the learning of functional or grammatical items. For example, you might give the learners sentence completion exercises or a guided composition requiring the writing of several examples of comparatives after you have presented and practised them orally. This can be very useful to clarify the grammar, to provide a change of activity in a lesson, or to give extra practice outside the classroom as homework.

The other main type of writing practice is intended to develop higher-level writing skills. That means the ability to do the writing tasks in intermediate and advanced proficiency examinations, and to do real business and academic writing. However, some work towards this type of writing can be started at lower levels. It can even be combined with writing principally intended to consolidate grammar.

Teaching ideas

Here are three examples of simple writing tasks:

- **Parallel compositions**
  With the whole class, discuss the topic of animals' characteristics and habits to elicit sentences in the Simple Present like:

  Chimpanzees live in central Africa. They eat fruit and leaves. Adult chimpanzees weigh 40 to 50 kilos. They are very intelligent animals.

  Ask for volunteers to write these sentences up on the board. Correct them if necessary. Then, telling the learners to use the sentences on the board as patterns, get them to work in pairs and write a parallel composition about some other animal, for example, kangaroos. You could then ask them to write compositions for homework about animals of their choice. Similar work could be done about cities (to practise 'There is/are') or famous people (to practise the Simple Past).

- **Parallel letters**
  Get the learners to read a letter, consisting mostly of personal information, from someone looking for a pen pal. Then tell them to write a reply with their own personal information, following the format of the original letter. The first paragraph might state the purpose of the letter, the second and third might give personal information, and the last paragraph might be a request for a reply. Another letter could ask for information about things to see and do in their city, or for information about a specific hotel.

- **Picture compositions**
  Get the learners to tell a simple story illustrated by a sequence of pictures, as in the example on the next page.

  Ask for volunteers to repeat the whole story from memory. Then get the learners to write the story in pairs or groups. It may be divided into three paragraphs—the beginning, the middle, and the end of the story.

To progress in the writing skill, intermediate learners need the same kind of practice as young native speakers. They need to read plenty of examples of good descriptive, narrative, and discursive writing, and develop the higher-level skills listed on page 96. Much of this work can be done in *lockstep* and pair or groupwork, rather than individually. For example, the whole class can brainstorm ideas on a topic. These can be written up on the board. Working in pairs or groups, the learners can then select the most relevant ideas and organize them into a sequence and then into sections and paragraphs. Different versions of this selection and organization can then be discussed in lockstep again. The general structure of introduction-body-conclusion can be established, with the body usually being the longest part of the text, often consisting of more than one paragraph. Pairs or groups can then write their final compositions in marker pen on large sheets of paper. These can be put up on the wall as an exhibition for the different pairs or groups to read and discuss. Attention should be directed first towards general organization and clarity. The correction of grammar, vocabulary, spelling, and punctuation errors should be dealt with separately. The main purpose of writing should be seen as achieving effective communication, not just producing correct English (although, of course, reasonably correct English is one element of effective communication).

Your feedback on individual composition work should also take a communicative approach. Say what you found interesting in the composition and how easy you found it to understand before you comment on any errors.

It is usually best to limit error correction to a manageable number of major errors only, and also to get learners to correct their own errors as far as possible. Depending on the individual ability of learners and the complexity of the errors, you can help learners correct their own work in different ways. For example:

- Simply underline easy-to-correct mistakes, or even put an exclamation mark in the margin by very obvious basic mistakes.

- For errors which are more difficult to correct, add a code for the type of error, which you have explained to the learners, for example:

  G   = grammar
  V   = vocabulary
  WO = word order
  Λ   = missing word
  SP = spelling
  P   = punctuation

- Partially make the correction for the learner to complete (for example, the learner wrote *arriving* instead of *arrival*, so you write _ _ _ _ *val*).

- Write in the correction for very hard-to-correct errors, especially with weaker learners.

Integrating skills

In our everyday use of language, we are continually integrating the language skills or switching from one skill to another. It is best to reflect this integration when teaching a second or foreign language. For example, good pre- or post-listening activities usually involve speaking, and sometimes reading and writing as well. Similarly, good pre- or post-reading activities usually involve listening and speaking, and sometimes writing. Speaking obviously usually involves listening, and sometimes reading (for example, an information-gap text). Writing may be handled orally first (for example, a picture composition, or brainstorming ideas), and may also involve reading as well, for example, reading a letter and writing a reply.

The integration of skills can be the basis for whole lesson plans. This is usually done by building the plan around a theme. Coursebooks often provide good material for this, which you can adapt or supplement in order to relate the theme more directly to your learners. The theme of traffic congestion in cities, for example, could be handled using listening and reading texts from the coursebook, plus the learners' own experiences of traffic jams for conversation. You could also get the learners to discuss and then write compositions about possible solutions for their own city, or for the country in general. You could even organize a 'public meeting' simulation with learners playing the roles of moderator, city mayor, head of police, head of public transport, President of the Drivers' Association, and President of the School Parents' Association.

One activity that can form a good basis for integrating skills is a project. The learners, working in groups, choose a topic they are interested in, and develop an extended piece of work, perhaps in the form of a poster or set of posters. A typical project might develop like this:

– Discussion and planning (speaking/listening/writing)
– Research and material collection (reading/writing)
– Evaluation and modification (reading/speaking/listening/writing)
– Production (writing/speaking/listening)
– Display and presentation (reading/speaking/listening).

The last stage, display and presentation, is vital to give a purpose to the project and motivate learners. Project work is one of the ways you can get close to a real communicative situation in the classroom. Also, all the learners can participate, no matter what their talents might be. Some like to read, others to speak in public, others to draw, and so on. Everyone can find satisfaction in using language in different ways to produce interesting and attractive pieces of work.

Summary

In Chapter 6 we have considered the following points:

Spoken and written language. Writing is usually more grammatically complete than speech. While spoken communication is supported by tone of voice, gesture, and context, a written text has to communicate through language alone. This usually means more carefully constructed sentences and a greater range of vocabulary and grammar. As a consequence, writing may often be more complex than speech. On the other hand, readers and writers can take their own time, for example, readers can reread difficult passages, and writers can plan and edit various drafts of a text.

Reading comprehension. Reading has much in common with listening, but the text is permanent, which may make it easier to understand. As with listening, our expectations and world knowledge, as well as our knowledge of the language, help us make sense of the text. Learners should be discouraged from reading—or translating—slowly word by word. Skimming and scanning are two approaches to reading which can be very useful for specific purposes (getting a general idea, or finding specific information). Full reading comprehension, which is needed for serious study or work, requires more knowledge of the language and higher-level reading skills. Like listening, reading is usually approached in three stages, pre-, while-, and post-reading. Reading in itself helps to develop the skills and language knowledge necessary for efficient comprehension. But most learners will read outside the classroom only if they have interesting texts available at their level.

Writing. Writing is the language skill used least by most people. It is also a skill usually learnt formally at school, and not handled well by many people, even in their L1. It involves low-level skills (handwriting or typing, spelling, constructing grammatical sentences, punctuating) and high-level cognitive skills (gathering ideas, organizing and sequencing, structuring, drafting, and editing). Most writing in elementary English courses is largely to consolidate language learning. This can be developed at higher levels into the composition of written texts (for example, stories, letters, and reports). A little real composition work can be started at lower levels with activities such as parallel compositions, parallel letters, and picture compositions. Composition work at higher levels can involve the whole class, or working in pairs or groups, as well as working individually. In your feedback, respond to the content and organization as well as the language. Involve learners in the correction of their own errors.

Integrating skills. This reflects natural use of the language and is therefore pedagogically useful. Most teaching of a specific skill involves the use of other skills. Whole lesson plans can integrate skills around a single theme or topic. Group projects also involve the use of all the skills. Integrated skills lessons and projects can be very interesting, enjoyable, and satisfying for the learners.

Project

Preparing an integrated communication skills sequence

Purpose: to develop the ability to promote integrated communication skills in learners.

Procedure:
1 Select a lesson from a widely-used coursebook that:
  a is built round a theme of potential interest to a group of learners you teach or know
  b contains a reasonably appropriate listening text on cassette.
2 Using the theme and the listening text as a basis, develop an integrated skills plan. You may want to use other material from the book as well as the listening text, for example, a reading text or a speaking activity, or you may prefer to use an authentic reading text from a magazine or book, or a speaking idea of your own.

3 If possible, use the plan and material with the group of learners you were thinking of.

4 If you are able to teach the plan, reflect afterwards on how it went, and what changes you would make if you were to use it again. If you are not able to teach the plan, leave it for a week without looking at it; then go through the plan and material, imagining any problems you might encounter and thinking how you could avoid them.

7 REVIEW AND REMEDIAL WORK

Introduction

In this chapter we look at the reasons why review and remedial work should be an integral part of teaching English. This relates both to the nature of the language learning process and the lack of sufficient use of the language in most classroom courses. We then present a range of review and clarification activities, and ideas for remedial work.

The need for review and remedial work

In most language courses there is far too little time for the intensive use of the language necessary for permanent learning, use similar to that of children acquiring their L1 or immigrants an L2. For this reason, most teachers and learners consider some review work necessary to reactivate, consolidate, and clarify previously presented language items. And most coursebooks include review units.

Also, errors are an integral part of language learning. They are not just evidence of failure to learn. Anyone who remembers how they learnt a foreign language is aware of how long it took them to eliminate certain elementary errors from their speaking and writing. Even advanced learners who are quite fluent usually have a number of fossilized errors in their English, for example *'He said me' instead of 'He told me', and leaving off the final 's' in the third person singular of the Present Tense. We have heard competent teachers of English, all with a level well above Cambridge First Certificate or 500 points in TOEFL, make this kind of error. Teachers are also human, simply learners who are further along the same road that their pupils are travelling. This should enable them to understand their pupils' situation very well.

All learners need an enormous amount of use of the language—which includes listening to English and thinking in English as well as speaking it—to really acquire its forms and functions. In situations where opportunities to use the language and receive feedback outside the classroom are limited, review and remedial work in the classroom become vital.

In spite of general agreement about the need for review and remedial work, teachers have different attitudes towards them, and so do learners. For some, review and remedial work are an unattractive or depressing part of language teaching and learning. They are associated with failure to learn properly, and often done just in preparation for tests. Teachers with this attitude may make review and remedial work seem like a constant, frustrating, and sometimes exasperating battle against the learners' dullness and laziness. Some teachers just repeat again and again the same explanations and practice that produced little success previously. However, other teachers consider review and remedial work an essential part of language teaching and learning, an integral part of the programme. They believe that repeated explanations and practice seldom produce better results the second or third time they are used than they did the first time. What is needed, they believe, is new work on old language. These teachers see review and remedial work as an interesting challenge, requiring ingenuity and creativity. The second view is more appropriate. Review and remedial work are essential parts of foreign language teaching and learning. To understand just how important they really are, it is useful to look at them in relation to the language learning process.

The language learning process

Language learning is a very complex process. It is possible here to present only some of the main ideas, strongly supported by theory and research, on what actually takes place when people learn a language. Apart from providing useful background for our discussion of review and remedial work, these ideas should illuminate many of the recommendations already given in this book.

Input, imitation, and cognitive hypotheses

Nobody learns a language without a lot of *input* through listening, and sometimes through reading. Learners may simply imitate bits of this input, usually imperfectly at first. They may also use it to develop 'cognitive hypotheses' about how the language works. Early hypotheses are often inaccurate, for example, a learner's statement, *'I putted it in the box'*, may be based on the mistaken hypothesis that in the Past Tense all verbs end in *-ed*. Instead of the large quantity of natural input available to children acquiring their L1, or immigrants acquiring an L2, classroom language learners are usually given a few models, an explanation, or an example and a translation. Then, instead of many opportunities to experiment through imitating and developing hypotheses, they are often expected to produce perfectly accurate sentences from the start. The reason for this is obviously partly to save time, which is a scarce commodity in most language courses. But the results usually show that it is virtually impossible to do without ample input and learning time. And by results, we are referring to what learners are able to do in normal conversation and written composition, not what they are able to do in formal exercises which focus on specific grammatical items.

Subconscious and conscious processes

Some subconscious learning may take place when language forms are just repeated again and again in drills. Many children learning their L1 repeat words and phrases over and over again, for example, talking to themselves while playing. But learning seems to be especially strong when language forms are used for real communication, not just repeated mechanically. The process of learning a language subconsciously while being exposed to it and using it in communication is generally referred to as 'language acquisition'. We sometimes notice things about the grammar or vocabulary of a language simply when using it for listening, reading, speaking, or writing. Some people are better at this than others. We also become aware of features of a language when consciously learning it, for example, doing 'grammar work' or 'vocabulary work'. This may be in class with a teacher, in a library, or at home with study materials and reference books. Conscious learning seems to be useful for adolescents and adults, but not usually for young children. They benefit mostly from repetition, for example, chanting and singing, and communicative practice, for example, stories and games. But acquisition opportunities through real communicative use of the language seem to be absolutely essential for all categories of learner.

Errors and learning

Errors are a natural, inevitable, and necessary part of learning. This is the case even when learning is successful, as in the case of children learning their L1 and most immigrants learning an L2. Children learning English as their L1 make errors very similar to those made by learners of English as a foreign language. At three or four years old, they produce utterances like these:

> It dirty. What your name? Where doggie gone? (missing article, missing auxiliary)
> He live with me. Mummy don't let me play. (missing third person singular 's')

Why it's not eating? What he will do? I didn't went. (incorrect interrogative forms, incorrect negative forms)
I putted it in the box. It's broked. This is gooder. (incorrect irregular forms)

After several years and thousands of hours of listening and speaking, children eventually learn the accepted forms and uses of their L1. The errors disappear, and the children become full members of their linguistic community. Relatively few adult immigrants succeed to the same extent. Usually, at least a trace of foreign accent and a few 'fossilized' errors indicate that they are not using their L1.

As well as having much less opportunity to hear and speak the new language than children acquiring their L1 or immigrants, learners of English in classrooms in their own country also have less real need for the language to motivate them. Some of their errors are very hard to eliminate. Errors in controlled language practice are less significant than those in communicative use of the language. It is relatively easy for learners to produce correct memorized language or slowly construct correct forms in controlled practice. But the best indication of how much of the language they have really acquired is in natural communication, in activities such as conversation and free composition. Then, they are not focusing on the language but on ideas.

Pedagogical and natural syllabuses

Teachers are usually expected to teach the Simple Present Tense one month, Frequency Adverbs the next month, the Comparative the next, and so on. If you do this, you may get most of your learners to do exercises satisfactorily and pass tests. But that does not mean that you have taught and they have learnt everything permanently or completely. Personal experience as well as research indicate that virtually all children learning their L1 as well as foreign language learners make mistakes in basic grammatical structures long after they first encounter the form concerned. Language acquisition is a long and complex process that rarely follows the syllabuses of classroom courses. There is conflict between pedagogical syllabuses, which concentrate on one thing at a time, and what is called 'the natural syllabus', which deals with everything mixed together naturally. You should not be shocked when your pupils make 'basic' mistakes in intermediate courses. It is perfectly normal. But it does require remedial action.

Variables

There are many differences in learning situations and in individual learners that affect the degree of success in language learning. Success tends to be much greater when there is high motivation. This may be *instrumental* (a real need for the language for study or work), *intrinsic* (enjoyment in learning the language), or *integrative* (a desire to be involved with native speakers of the language and their culture). Actual or potential motivation needs to be recognized and promoted by teachers.

Success also tends to be greater when the individual characteristics of learners are taken into account. Some learners are more 'visual' (they prefer seeing written examples of the language) and others are more 'aural' (they prefer working with the spoken language). Some learners are more 'communicative' (they prefer conversational activities) and others are more 'analytical' (they prefer focusing on grammar). You should try to offer a variety of activities in your classes to suit all these different types of learner.

Success also tends to be much greater when learner autonomy is developed. That means helping the learners to learn without your help, as they will have to once they begin to use the language and continue to learn it outside the classroom.

Implications for review and remedial work

What are the implications for review and remedial work of these ideas concerning the language learning process?

Use varied, and appropriate activities

Do not just repeat grammatical explanations and drills. Use a variety of review and remedial activities appropriate for the level and age of the learners. Include work with listening and reading texts, and activities where the main focus is on communication.

Get learner output, and provide feedback

Use some activities requiring output from the learners, including a good deal of free production in communication. Provide appropriate feedback on output. Remember that some of this feedback may come from other learners or from the learner who produced the output.

Work with natural, mixed language

Do some review and remedial work with mixed grammar, not always focusing on a single structure or area of grammar.

Be patient and positive

Never show frustration or exasperation, even when the learners get very basic things wrong or cannot remember them. But try to establish clear and realistic objectives, and involve the learners in achieving these.

Make review and remedial work enjoyable and satisfying

Try to make review and remedial work as interesting and challenging as any other work in the course, taking into account learner motivation and differences. Show your pleasure at their successes. Promote learner autonomy as much as possible, for example, with self-correction, and pair and groupwork.

Review activities

Review and remedial work should be a regular part of your teaching. Activities should depend on the level and age of the learners, the language points you are dealing with, and the time available.

Teaching ideas

The ideas that follow are just some examples of grammar and vocabulary review activities.

- **Recall**
  Ask the learners to remember what types and uses of sentences they have encountered in the course in the last week or month. In pairs or groups, get them to write examples, naming the forms and uses if they can, for example, 'Past Simple', 'Comparative', or 'Conditional'. Then elicit examples from different pairs or groups, write them on the board, and get the learners to decide whether the examples are correct or not.

- **Structure recognition**
  Prepare about eight sentences, half of them illustrating one structure, and the other half a different structure. For example, you could contrast the Simple Past and Present Perfect tenses:

  1 They went to France for their holiday.
  2 She has taken French classes for two years now.
  3 He has read several books about French cuisine this year.
  4 They stayed in an old castle on the Loire.
  5 They ate the most delicious food.
  6 They have decorated their living room with posters of the castle and the Loire.

Then, tell the learners to decide in pairs which sentences belong to one group, and which to the other. Discuss the reasons for their decisions, that is, the key features or rules they noticed.

In the example, numbers 1, 4, 5 are Simple Past, and numbers 2, 3, and 6 are Present Perfect. The Simple Past has a single verb in the affirmative, sometimes regular (for example, 'stayed') and sometimes irregular (for example, 'went', and 'ate'). The Present Perfect has the auxiliary verb 'have' plus the past participle, sometimes regular (for example, 'decorated'), sometimes irregular like the Past (for example, 'read'), and sometimes irregular and different from the Past (for example, 'taken').

You can mix more than two, different structures, for example, First, Second, and Third Conditionals.

- **Underlining examples**
  Get learners to read a text and underline all the examples of one or more structures under review. Then, in pairs, get them to check which sentences they have underlined and discuss how they recognized the structures, and how they function. Then check with the whole class.

- **Unscrambling items**
  Mix up the sentences of two or three texts (best on a prepared handout, not laboriously written up on the board). Then get learners in pairs to write out the texts separately. Here is an example:

  1 One morning, David got up much earlier than usual.
  2 Jim always gets up at exactly six-fifteen.
  3 He had a quick shower and left the house without having breakfast.
  4 Sam has travelled more than anyone else in his class.
  5 When he got to the university, he went straight to the library.
  6 He likes to take things in a calm, organized way.
  7 He has been to Disneyland in the west, and Corfu in the east.
  8 He hates to be in a hurry.
  9 He wanted to see Mary, the librarian.
  10 He has hopes of being an airline pilot—a very punctual and reliable one.
  11 However, he has never visited a single museum in his own city.
  12 Unfortunately, she didn't go to work that day.

In this example, one text is Simple Past (sentences 1, 3, 5, 9, and 12); one is Simple Present (sentences 2, 6, 8, and 10), and one is Present Perfect (sentences 4, 7, and 11). The learners should discover this for themselves. The meaning of the sentences will help them.

- **Grammar summary tables**

  Another useful review task that is easy to organize, is the completion of grammar summary tables. These can be adapted from coursebook grammar tables, for example:

What	_____	you	do?
	_____	she	
	_____	they	

I	_____	_____	student.
She	_____	_____	architect.
They	_____		carpenters.

  Completing a grammar task like this is usually much better for learners than being shown a grammar table or being told the rules once again by you. It is more interesting and memorable for them, and therefore more effective.

- **Guided compositions**

  Get the learners in pairs or groups to write a story or text on the basis of key words, for example:

  John—Mary—neighbours—gardens—cat—pond—fish—bones—piranhas—wall

  This set of key words should produce plenty of examples of the Past Simple.

  Pictures can also be used—see the examples opposite.

  This pair of pictures should produce plenty of examples of Comparatives.

  If the learners are working in groups, the compositions can be written with marker pens on large sheets of paper. These can be put on the wall so that the other groups can read them. The learners can then comment on any changes they consider are necessary.

- **Whispers**

  'Whispers' is a sentence grammar game. Organize the learners into teams on lines of chairs from the back of the room to the front. The learners at the back of each line come to the front and memorize a sentence that you show them written on a card. The sentences you use can be of recently studied structures, or basic structures that learners are having difficulty remembering. They then run back to their place and whisper the sentence to the learner in front of them, who whispers it to the learner in front, and so on. Finally, the learner at the front of the line writes the sentence on the board, which has been divided into sections for each team.

Wait until all the teams have finished, noting the order in which they finished. Then check the sentences with the class. The first team with the sentence correct, or the best approximation to the correct sentence wins. You can play several rounds with different sentences and different structures. The sentences can even build up into a very short story or text, so that the growing context helps the learners understand later sentences and the whole activity becomes more communicative.

- **Integrated skills sessions**
  Whole review lessons can be planned as integrated skills sessions, moving, for example, from reading to discussion to listening to role play and finally to writing.

The whole session can require the use of one structure, for example, Simple Past. Or you can move from one structure to another, for example, beginning with reading and discussion about two alternative holiday resorts (Comparative forms), then moving to the presentation of holiday plans ('Going to' Future), reports after imaginary holidays (Simple Past), and so on. Periodically, you can focus the learners' attention on the structures being practised.

Of course, this kind of session is possible only if you have sufficient time, as well as a collaborative group. You also need time and creativity to prepare such a session yourself. However, some coursebooks have review lessons designed in this way, and you may be able to adapt them easily to your specific situation.

Remedial work

Remedial work on persistent problems should be done as needed, not on a regular basis like review work. It should be based on your evaluation of learners' problems and identification of specific errors and mistakes. This evaluation is best done by constantly monitoring the learners' performance and noting recurrent errors and mistakes, especially those that occur in fluency work. Remember, the fact that learners can produce certain grammatical structures in accuracy practice or written exercises does not mean that they can do so in more communicative activities.

It is worth mentioning here that a distinction is generally made between errors, mistakes, and slips. *Errors* are incorrect forms or uses that occur because the learner simply does not know what the appropriate form or use is. He or she needs to become aware or be informed of what is right and wrong. *Mistakes* are incorrect forms or uses that occur in spite of the learner knowing the appropriate form or use. The learner needs to notice mistakes more, and convert conscious knowledge into automatic or unconsciously produced performance. *Slips* are just like slips of the tongue of native speakers. They are of little or no significance.

Remedial work should focus on recurrent or persistent mistakes. It should also pay attention to errors that indicate important gaps in the learners' English or persistent misconceptions about English. Persistently used incorrect forms are generally referred to as *fossilized* errors. In fact they may be 'fossilized errors' (the learner thinks they are correct) or 'fossilized mistakes' (the learner actually knows the correct form and can self-correct).

In remedial work you need to distinguish between general problems and those of individual learners. General problems require attention in class, but individual problems are often best handled after class and through individualized homework. One of the best general principles in remedial work is never to do for learners what they can do for themselves. Learners must notice mistakes or errors, and discover for themselves what is wrong and right if they are really going to overcome their problems.

Teaching ideas

Here are some ideas for remedial work:

- **Noticing and correcting mistakes**
  Select some of the most common and significant mistakes your learners make. Write on the board sentences the learners themselves have produced in oral or written work containing these mistakes. Include one or two perfectly correct sentences, also produced by the learners. Keep all the sentences anonymous. Ask the learners, working in pairs, to identify the sentences with mistakes, decide what exactly is wrong, and correct them. Then check with the whole class and discuss the mistakes and the rules.

  Similar noticing and correcting can be done with specially prepared texts in which you introduce some typical mistakes.

  Another strategy is to establish 'the mistake of the week' on Monday. It should be a significant mistake that most learners sometimes make and that many learners make frequently. Every time someone makes that particular mistake, the other learners should raise their hands. Note who raises their hand first and congratulate them. Of course, the learner who makes the mistake can raise his or her own hand—we often notice our mistakes the moment we have made them.

- **Drilling**
  The repetition of the same structure does not have to be mechanical and boring, and it can be a useful remedial technique. It is useful because some mistakes seem to be the result of strong habits, and to break a bad habit we need to replace it with a good one. You can make drilling fun by using songs, verses, and rap-like chanting. You will need to select, adapt, or create material to do this. You can also make it like a game: for remedial drilling of the Past negative, you say 'We went to England' and every learner has to say what they *didn't* do or what *didn't* happen there, without repeating a sentence, for example:

Learner 1	I didn't see the Queen.
Learner 2	It didn't rain.
Learner 3	I didn't play soccer.

If the learners run out of ideas, you can change to another country. You can even make it a competition, with learners from two teams alternating. The team that produces the last sentence wins.

- **Mental drilling**
  Drilling does not have to be out loud. Learners can do it silently, in their heads. Suggest to learners who repeatedly say, for example, *'must to + verb' instead of 'must + verb' that they repeat in their heads when they have a spare moment: 'I must do my homework'; 'I must telephone Elisa'; 'I must. . .'. This can be done on the bus, driving, or walking. In the next class, you could ask them for some examples of what they 'must do'.

- **Auction**
  Show the learners a poster with six to eight carefully selected sentences on it, about half of which are correct and half incorrect. Tell them not to discuss or say anything about the sentences. Explain that you will auction the sentences (like an auction of paintings or antiques). Each learner—or pair of learners—starts with $300 capital, and can bid $100, $200, or $300 for the sentences they think are correct. For example:

Teacher	Right. Look at Sentence A—a beautiful sentence. Who would like to start with $100? Anybody?
Learner 1	$300!
Teacher	Ah, you're really convinced it's a good sentence. Right, so Sentence A goes to Omar for $300. Well, that's all your money, Omar. Now, any bids for Sentence B, another beauty?
Learner 2	$100!
Teacher	Good, $100 from Rebecca. Any advance on $100? No . . .? OK, going . . . going . . . gone to Rebecca for $100, a real bargain. Now . . .

  When you have finished the auction, get the learners to discuss in groups which sentences were in fact correct and which were not. Then check with the whole class.

Personalized remedial work

Individual differences tend to increase as learners progress. At beginner level most learners' problems are very similar. At higher levels, learners' strengths and weaknesses usually become more differentiated, sometimes resulting in very heterogeneous classes. They are no longer all close to the pedagogical syllabus, but at different stages of their own 'natural syllabuses'.

Learners should be encouraged to take as much responsibility as possible for their own learning, and especially for remedial work. You can help, suggesting, for example, 'mental drilling', extra exercises for homework, or the rewriting of marked compositions, but they themselves must do the work. And if you have self-access facilities in your institution, you can direct learners to appropriate activities there.

Written composition work is one of the best opportunities for you to attend to the learners' more individual needs. Your feedback on written compositions can include:

– Comments that show you understand the process they are going through—their successes as well as their problems.
– A coding system for errors, like the one on page 99, that helps them notice and correct their own mistakes.
– Comments and exercises on areas of language where they make repeated mistakes or errors. For example, if a learner repeatedly produces sentences like 'I want that my children succeed in life', you could write:

I want <u>you to</u> avoid a mistake you often make, Homero. For that reason, I would like <u>you to</u> complete the following exercise:

1 The policeman wanted ⎯⎯⎯⎯⎯⎯⎯⎯⎯⎯. (the driver, stop)
2 She would like ⎯⎯⎯⎯⎯⎯⎯⎯. (her children, speak English)
3 They asked ⎯⎯⎯⎯⎯⎯⎯. (John, wait outside)
4 He told ⎯⎯⎯⎯⎯⎯. (me, sit down)
5 I prefer ⎯⎯⎯⎯⎯⎯. (you, correct your own mistakes)

In the final analysis, most language teaching needs to be personalized in some way. But you can only assist the learners. The actual learning has to be done by the learners themselves, in their own heads. Eventually, every learner must take responsibility for his or her own language learning, although of course, they need all the help you can give them. Paradoxically, that often means not helping them too much.

Summary

In Chapter 7 we have considered the following points:

The need for review and remedial work. In most courses there is insufficient practice, and learners forget old language items while learning new ones. Also, absolutely everyone makes mistakes while learning. In fact, most people (including language teachers) continue to make elementary mistakes for a very long time. For these reasons, most teachers, learners, and coursebook writers accept the need for some review and remedial work. However, some teachers feel exasperated by it, while others approach it positively. A positive approach is obviously better, and it is easier to be positive when you understand some important things about the language learning process.

The language learning process. Language learning is complex. It requires more language input than most classroom learners get. The models and explanations used to try to save time in the classroom cannot fully substitute this necessary input. And controlled practice and teacher correction cannot substitute the ample free experimentation learners need, imitating and hypothesizing about the English they hear. Most learners benefit from opportunities to learn subconsciously as well as consciously, like children acquiring their L1. Errors are natural, inevitable, and necessary in all language learning. Errors in free conversation and composition indicate the stage a learner is at much better than errors in controlled exercises. Language learning is also a longer and more erratic process than most syllabuses recognize. One reason for this is that it is strongly affected by variables, for example, motivation and individual learner differences. There are clear implications for teaching, and especially for review and remedial work. These include being patient and positive, and making review and remedial work enjoyable and satisfying.

Review activities. These should be a regular part of your teaching. Among the wide range of possible activities are recall, recognition or discovery activities, guided compositions, and integrated skills sessions.

Remedial work. This should be done as needed. The emphasis should be on helping the learners to help themselves. Again there is a wide range of possible activities, for example, noticing and correcting mistakes, mental drilling, and personalized remedial work (for example, feedback on compositions).

Project

Preparing review activities

Purpose: to develop the ability to prepare review activities.

Procedure:

1 Study the examples in this chapter of the following types of review activities: Structure recognition (page 108), Unscrambling items (page 109), and Grammar summary tables (page 110).

2 Design one activity of each type for different language points, for example, 'There is/are', Comparatives/Superlatives, Conditionals.

3 If you are able to use some of your activities with learners, do so and evaluate the response of the learners and the effectiveness of the activities. If you are not able to use your activities, leave them for a week and then look at them again critically.

8 PLANNING AND MANAGING CLASSES

Introduction

In this chapter, we look first at long-term planning of classes. This usually follows some kind of syllabus divided into units. The syllabus is the basis of a course, though it may need adapting, for example, to a specific teaching situation. Short-term organization is then discussed, and we present one possible format for lesson planning. Effective class management is essential for actual teaching, and we offer suggestions. Finally, we consider approaches to two specific teaching situations—children's courses and large groups.

Long-term planning

Courses are normally based on a syllabus. This may be a document prepared by your school or educational authority, or it may be the contents section of your coursebook (see Chapter 9). The syllabus constitutes your essential guide for the course. It sets your objectives and tells you what to teach, in what order, in what period of time, and—to some extent—how.

The course syllabus

At first sight, a syllabus can seem distant from the daily task of preparing and giving individual lessons. It usually contains a long list of items and activities for up to a year's work. There may also be general methodological indications, and these may not necessarily suit your teaching style or your specific teaching situation very well. However, the syllabus is the starting point for all your more detailed planning of lessons. Your lesson planning and what you actually do in the classroom must take into account the major goals, the unit divisions, and the general methodological indications of your syllabus. Table 8.1 shows the different levels of planning.

Document	Focus	Time scale
course syllabus	level and goals	year/semester
syllabus unit	block of work	month/set number of weeks
work plan	teaching cycle	week
lesson plan	specific actions	day

Table 8.1: Levels of planning in a syllabus

Before you can begin to make any detailed plan you need to be familiar with the main goals, general objectives, and content of the syllabus. That includes understanding:

– what the learners are expected to know and be able to do in English at the beginning of the course, and at the end of the course.
– what the roles of grammar, functions, topics, and skills are. Some syllabuses may give more emphasis to language knowledge and others to communication skills.

If your syllabus is not clear about levels of learner performance and major goals, you need to take steps to clarify these. For example, you may need to consult a co-ordinator or senior teacher, examine the coursebook in detail, and look at any course tests that exist. You may sometimes even need to take your own decisions.

An important consideration is whether the syllabus and the course material allows for constant reactivation and integration of previously introduced items and skills. To achieve this, many modern syllabuses are not linear, but spiral. A linear syllabus may mean, for example, a week of 'There is/are' and only 'There is/are', then a week of Possessives and only Possessives, then a week of Likes/Dislikes and only Likes/Dislikes, and then a Review of 'There is/are', Possessives, and Likes/Dislikes. The Review may well reveal that the learners have half-forgotten 'There is/are' during the two weeks they have not practised it, and are already beginning to forget Possessives. In contrast, a spiral syllabus constantly tries to reactivate previously introduced language and skills, and to integrate new items into a growing repertoire of English. It is similar to Figure 1.3, presented in Chapter 1.

As we emphasized in Chapter 7, learners quickly forget items they do not use. Also, isolated language items (such as 'There is/are') are not much use in dynamic communication situations. To be able to communicate, learners need to develop a growing repertoire of language which is available whenever required. If your syllabus appears to be strongly linear, it is a good idea to include some regular reactivation and integration sessions in your lessons. You can give a little time to such work every lesson, and perhaps also spend longer on it once a week, for example, every Friday.

Syllabus units

The unit divisions of a syllabus usually indicate how the content can be grouped together, and how fast the course should move. A unit may have a single theme, for example, 'Talking about the future' or 'Space travel'. A theme, or some other association between the language elements, can help the learners remember what they have been working on better. The move from unit to unit can also give both you and the learners a sense of progress over the many weeks or months of the course.

Units are also usually related to periods of time. For example, you may have to cover a unit every month, or every ten teaching hours. This should help you relate the syllabus to your specific teaching conditions and learners. If you are lucky, you may find you have plenty of time for the relaxed use of materials and activities that are particularly interesting and useful for your group. If you are less fortunate, you may find that you need to be extremely organized, disciplined, and creative to cover just the most essential objectives and content of the syllabus without driving the learners to despair.

To save time, some teachers omit the review units in their coursebook. This is not advisable unless you have managed to incorporate reactivation and integration sessions into your regular teaching. It is essential to keep alive the language and skills from earlier in the course, and from previous courses. An adequate syllabus allows for the fact that learners will be accumulating knowledge and skills, learning new things without forgetting old ones. The saying 'More haste, less speed' is relevant here. Teachers often think they are going faster and that learners are making more progress when they constantly move on to new language items and skills. It may seem that spending lessons on what the learners have 'already studied' is wasting time. But in reality, the only way learners make genuine progress in learning language, and being able to communicate with it, is by constantly using it.

Short-term planning

Short-term planning may involve work plans covering a week's teaching as well as individual lesson plans.

Work plans

Work plans consist of the outlines of a sequence of lessons. They should provide your teaching with continuity and coherence. This is hard to achieve when looking at each lesson in isolation. Work plans can ensure that, over each week, there is variety in your teaching, something for every type of learner. They can also ensure that you are achieving the balance between old and new language items, accuracy and fluency practice, and language and skills work, and that you do not lose sight of your main goal, communication. If, out of three lessons per week, one consists largely of presentation and practice of new language items, at least one other lesson each week should consist largely of communicative work.

Lesson planning

For truly professional teachers, lesson planning is not optional, it is essential preparation for teaching. It is a matter of deciding exactly what you are going to teach, and how. Unless you establish your objectives and activities in this way, you may find yourself just going mechanically through the coursebook, or trying to improvise whole lessons. Such approaches usually produce poor results, although some improvisation and flexibility is good, even essential, in teaching. Learners can easily notice the difference between teachers who plan and those who do not. And if their teacher does not make an effort, why should they?

To begin your lesson plan, decide where the lesson fits into your week's work plan or teaching cycle. Then establish specific objectives for the lesson. These will largely be determined by the phase in the teaching cycle. Here are some examples of lesson objectives:

- To present and achieve controlled production of a new grammatical-functional item.
- To achieve guided communicative use of a new item.
- To achieve the communicative use of a mixed range of language in writing.
- To promote the learners' confidence in the conversational use of English.
- To develop comprehension of public announcements.

You can develop your objectives and the activities to achieve them using the recommendations in the appropriate sections of this book, for example, Chapter 2 for the presentation of new functional-grammatical items, and Chapter 5 for the development of speaking skills.

The activities and materials should be appropriate for your objectives, and also for your specific group of learners. When deciding on appropriate activities and materials, take into account the learners' age, interests, and abilities. Calculate the approximate time for each activity so that you do not end up doing only half of what you planned, or having no plan for the last quarter of the lesson. And remember that there needs to be a variety of activity and interaction, for example, between lockstep, pairwork, groupwork, and individual work.

Here is a typical lesson plan:

Group: 3B
Room: 7
Unit: 8
Time: 8–9.00 p.m.
Date: 8th April

Objectives/teaching points: Fluency/consolidation practice of Present Perfect (presentation/accuracy practice last class) combined with Simple Past. Development of conversation and listening skills.

Specific objectives/ activities	Materials/aids	Procedures/ interactions	Time
1 To warm up LL, establish topic, get conversation practice: Discussion of holiday activities	Photos of snorkelling, water-skiing, horse riding, etc.	TQ–LA Have you ever _____ed? Where/When? → PRS	5'
2 To establish holiday discussion situation, give listening practice, lead into main activity: Listening to friends discussing their holiday plans	Cassette 23.7 Table on board for lists of activities	Task 1: *Who wants to go to Scotland? Who wants to go to the Costa Brava? Why?* Task 2: List things to do in Scotland and the Costa Brava	10'
3 To get LL to use Pres. Perf. + Past in free conversation: GPS of three agree on holiday destination, give reasons	Poster with choice of holiday resorts, things to do in each	T and L model conversation similar to cassette → GPS of three, instructions to note reasons for decision: *Yuri has been to . . . , and he doesn't want to go again. Ana has seen a bullfight and didn't like it. Bogdan has never . . .*	15'

4 To check use of Pres. Perf. and Past: GP reports	Same poster	Representative of each GP reports to class: *We decided to go to* _____ *because . . . ; We decided not to go to* _____ *because . . .*	15'
5 To clarify use of Pres. Perf., wind down: Dialogue fill-in	Handout: dialogue fill-in	IND fill-in → Check in PRS → Check on board	10'

Homework: Holiday composition

Key: T = teacher; TQ = teacher questions; L(L) = learner(s); LA = learner answers; PRS = pairs; GP(S) = group(s); IND = individual; → leads to/followed by

The main elements and considerations in the above plan are:

- Clear stages: warm-up (1); lead-in (2); main activity (3); follow-up (4); and wind-down (5)—and smooth transitions between them.
- A unifying theme, running through the conversation, listening, and writing activities.
- Appropriate relationships between objectives, activities, materials, and procedures.
- Attention to both the communicative use of English and formal correctness in the language, i.e. fluency and accuracy.
- Consideration of the learners' interests and the learning conditions, as well as the grammatical-functional items in the syllabus.

The stages and transitions give a comfortable flow to the lesson. Each stage requires different behaviour from the teacher, a different level of effort from the learners, and changes in pace. A spare activity—for example, a game or quiz—could have been included at the end in case the lesson went faster than anticipated. The learners are provided with enough input—photos, a model conversation on cassette, and a poster—to get them going, but they are also given the opportunity to use their personal experience in realistic tasks. The interest of the topic and tasks, the changes of activity and interaction, and the relatively relaxed pace, should help the learners through this late class— 8.00 to 9.00 in the evening.

Obviously, lesson plans need to vary according to the age and level of the learners, the objectives, the time of day, and even the time of year. Young learners need more changes of activity and more physical activity. They have much shorter attention spans than older learners, and can get very restless.

Older learners at higher levels can sometimes work enthusiastically at the same task for quite long periods of time. Lessons at the end of a long morning, the end of a long day, or just before a holiday period, need to be lighter than other lessons.

During or after a lesson you can make a few notes on the plan, and it will then act as the starting point for the following lesson plan. A book, folder, or file of such plans can be a permanent record of the progress achieved with a particular group, and may serve as the basis for even better plans next time you teach the course.

Class management

You cannot plan everything that will happen in a lesson. You need strategies to respond to actual events, including unexpected ones. But if the learners have become accustomed to certain patterns of behaviour, your classes will run more smoothly.

Getting attention and participation

It is unrealistic and undesirable to expect the learners to pay attention to you throughout a lesson. But you should be able to get their attention fairly quickly when you need it. If, for example, you cannot get everybody's attention when giving instructions or explanations, serious problems may result. You may find yourself explaining something over and over again to individuals or groups of learners. At worst, the lesson may even disintegrate into chaos. Shouting louder and louder is seldom an effective solution. And it is bad for your relationship with the learners, your general mood, and of course, your voice. You need to train the learners to respond to a range of non-verbal signals, for example:

- Stand with your hand raised until you have total silence and everybody's attention. You can train the learners to raise their hands too, and attend to you as soon as they see you with your hand raised.
- Signal that one or more learners should come to the front of the class. This tends to make the others curious.
- Point at your watch to indicate that you are about to end an activity.

Interest is usually the best way to attract and hold attention, and to get voluntary participation. Classroom atmosphere is also very important. You can compel participation in lockstep practice with your questions (for example, 'What's the capital of France . . . Mario?') and instructions (for example, 'Question . . . Sandra, answer . . . Robert'). But voluntary participation in lockstep work, and more especially in pair and groupwork, will usually be poor unless the topics interest the learners, and you encourage rather than criticize them.

Giving and checking instructions

Effective instructions are vital if activities are to go well, especially activities involving changes of interaction, for example, from lockstep to pairwork. A communicative approach to language teaching requires some quite complicated activities and interactions, and this means you need to have all the learners' attention when giving instructions. You need to train them to be quiet and listen very carefully. This is especially the case if you are giving instructions in English. (You may remember that in Chapter 1 we said English should be used for communication in the classroom as much as possible.)

Think about both what you are going to say, and how you are going to say it. Instructions should be simple and clear, and, as far as possible, standardized. Try always to use the same type of instructions and language for the same type of routine activities. However, especially with elementary learners, even simple, clear, familiar language is not always sufficient to get complex messages across. The learners may need a demonstration of the activity as well. Several examples of this technique have been given in previous chapters, and there is one at stage 3 of the lesson plan above: 'T and L model conversation similar to cassette'. The activity might actually be organized like this:

Extract 1

Teacher	Now, I want you to discuss holiday plans in the same way as they did in the conversation on the cassette. Work in groups of three. Discuss every choice, and note reasons for and against each one. First, copy this table from the board. OK? What are you going to do right now, Andrei?
Learner	Copy the table from the board.
Teacher	Right. Copy it, everyone. [*Pause while learners copy table.*] OK. Have you finished?
Learners	Yes.
Teacher	Good. Now listen to Ana, Yuri, and me. Come up here, Ana, Yuri. Right. Now, what about Venice? I've never been there. [*T, whose name is Boris, writes 'Boris never been' in the 'for' column under Venice.*]
Learner	I've been there. It rained all the time. It was very sad. [*T writes 'Yuri been—rain—sad' in the 'against' column under Venice.*]
Teacher	What about you, Ana? [*Ana gives a reason for or against.*] What about Paris? [*Reasons for and against going to Paris are added to the table.*] OK? You get the idea? In groups of three, discuss holiday plans. Discuss every option. Note

	reasons for and against each option in the table. You'll have 15 minutes. What do you have to do, Nikolai?
Learner	In groups of three we discuss holiday plans . . .
Teacher	Right. And . . . , Martina?
Learner	We discuss every option . . .
Teacher	Right. And . . . , Vladimir?
Learner	We note the reasons for and against each option in the table.
Teacher	Right. How long do you have, Natasha?
Learner	15 minutes.
Teacher	Very good! Right, you can start . . . groups of three.

Never assume that the learners have understood what you want them to do just from the instructions. You need to make sure your message is perfectly clear. To check comprehension, you may ask selected learners to demonstrate the activity briefly, or paraphrase the instructions you have given. If necessary, you can even get learners to translate the instructions into their L1. They will soon get used to the idea that you will call on them to participate actively when you are setting up an activity. There may be occasions when it is best to explain something complicated or very new for the learners in their L1. Although our general recommendation is to avoid the use of L1 as much as possible, you should not feel that it is never to be used at all.

Managing pair and groupwork

There are, it is true, difficulties and risks associated with pair and groupwork, for example:

- the learners may be confused about the task and not do it properly
- the noise level may rise (though seldom more than in choral repetition)
- the learners may start talking about whatever they like in their L1
- the learners may make and repeat many errors
- you may not be able to get the learners' attention again and lose control of the class.

However, you can usually avoid these potential problems by careful preparation and organization, and by progressively training the learners to participate fully and effectively. If these things are done, the advantages of pair and groupwork far outweigh the drawbacks. For example, they provide:

- variety and dynamism
- an enormous increase in individual practice
- low-stress private practice
- opportunities to develop learner autonomy
- interaction with peers.

Introduce learners to pair and groupwork with very simple, clear, and brief tasks. By 'brief' we mean tasks that take only one or two minutes. For example, you can get learners to ask and answer in pairs the questions that they have just been practising in lockstep. Once they have done this kind of simple task successfully, they can move on to progressively longer, more complex, and freer tasks.

Other techniques and strategies that can make pair and groupwork as trouble-free and profitable as possible are:

- Set up the task in as in Extract 1 on page 129, i.e. give clear instructions followed by a demonstration and a comprehension check.
- Monitor the activity: move among the pairs or groups as quickly as possible, listening for major problems and helping the learners when necessary. Your 'ubiquitous presence' will deter the learners from using their L1.
- Train the learners to stop talking when you give a certain signal, for example, a raised hand.
- Check on the task after the pairs or groups have completed it, getting selected learners to give examples of what they said, or report on what they did.
- After the pair or groupwork, deal with major errors you noted: give spoken examples or write examples on the board for the learners to correct.
- Tell particularly noisy, uncooperative classes you will do pair and groupwork with them only if they keep their voices down and follow your instructions. The prospect of lessons with nothing but lockstep work is usually enough to get their co-operation.

Figure 8.1 shows useful stages in the management of pair or groupwork.

pre-task ⇨	task ⇨	post-task ⇨	follow-up
T outlines situation and gives instructions, followed by a comprehnsion check and a demonstration.	LL work in pairs or groups. T monitors, notes problems, and helps where necessary.	T signals to end the task and does a post-task check.	T deals with error-correction if necesary.

Figure 8.1: Stages in the management of pair or groupwork

As the learners acquire experience in working in pairs and groups, and achieve success, they usually begin to work better and enjoy the work more. They may soon find a lesson without pair or groupwork strange—even unsatisfactory. Pair and groupwork then becomes much easier for you to handle. But you should never forget the care needed to make a task work well.

Teacher and learner roles

Both teachers and learners need to play varying roles. You should be consciously aware of this. At different times, you need to:

- Present new information, control accuracy practice from the front, and make sure that as many learners as possible participate in the class and that most errors are corrected.
- Organize and facilitate lockstep fluency and skills activities from the front, encouraging voluntary participation and ignoring most errors.
- Monitor individual, pair, or group activities, moving around among the learners and helping and encouraging them.
- Inform the learners about their progress, trying to combine encouragement with honest evaluation and useful feedback.

These different roles require skill, confidence, and sensitivity.

At different times, the learners need to:

- Attend to information you give them, imitate your models, and try to do exactly as you indicate.
- Volunteer original ideas and ask relevant questions.
- Work with other learners, solving problems co-operatively.
- Work independently in class or at home, taking full responsibility for their own performance and learning.

It is, of course, your responsibility to make sure that you behave in the right way at the right time. It is also your responsibility to encourage the learners to behave appropriately, according to the activity and interaction they are involved in. If you are successful, the teaching–learning process will progress well and both the learners and you will feel confident working together.

Discipline

Discipline is the main preoccupation of some teachers, especially teachers of groups of children and adolescents. Other teachers hardly have to worry about it at all. Good order, co-operation, and respect in the classroom are seldom accidental. They are usually the direct result of the way you teach and the way you relate to the learners.

It is wise to begin some courses in a fairly formal or even strict way, and relax little by little as you gain the co-operation of the group. But you may soon start having problems if you do not follow these basic recommendations:

- Plan lessons, and include varied activities and interactions that keep the learners busy.
- Use topics and activities that you think will be interesting and enjoyable for the learners.
- Motivate the learners by focusing on what they do satisfactorily or well more than on what they do badly.
- Try to create a sense of community in the group.
- Be fair to all the learners, never favouring some over others.
- Show that you respect and are interested in all the learners as people, irrespective of how good they are at English.

In spite of every precaution and effort on your part, there is occasionally a learner or a group of learners in a class who seem determined to make trouble. If you have most of the learners on your side, it is much easier to handle such situations. Nevertheless, you may need to use some kind of punishment or report a troublemaker to the school principal. If so, it is important that the teacher–learner relationship does not break down completely. Never give a punishment that is humiliating or unreasonable, and always reintegrate learners into the group after they have received a reprimand or punishment. This is important not just for the learner involved, but also for your standing with the group. Groups almost always evaluate disciplinary action taken against one of their members. If the group feels that the punishment was unfair, or that you were unable to cope, the problem will only grow. It is also useful to develop your sense of humour. This is usually appreciated by others, and can help you face small and sometimes large problems.

Different teaching situations

There are some aspects of teaching that are specific to certain situations, and that have implications for planning and class management. Two of these situations are childrens' courses and large groups.

Children's courses

Young children, say up to the age of seven, find it difficult or impossible to see language as an abstract system, independent of communication or enjoyable sound sequences such as songs and rhymes. The highlighting of key grammatical features or elicitation of parallel sentences is wasted on them. They also find it difficult or impossible to think in terms of learning goals, although they respond to more immediate objectives such as drawing a picture or making a kite. They also find it difficult or impossible to work at one task for a long time. Their attention span is usually short, and they need frequent changes of activity. Finally, young children respond much better to affection than to discipline. They see most adults as potential 'aunts' and 'uncles'—or as 'ogres' they distrust and fear.

This tendency to see to the world in concrete and subjective terms, and to work at tasks for only short periods of time, begins to change significantly from about the age of about seven. By the age of ten, most children have begun to understand abstract systems, can establish learning goals to some extent, can complete fairly long tasks, and are beginning to make objective judgements of people.

There are important implications for teaching children. The younger the children, the more your lesson plans should consist of games, vocabulary linked to pictures and realia, manual activities such as drawing and colouring, songs and rhymes, and stories. Your lesson plans should also contain frequent changes of activity. Finally, it is important to maintain a good rapport with children, and to foster an affectionate and co-operative atmosphere.

Large groups

The basic principles of teaching English are the same for groups of fourteen, forty, fifty, or sixty learners. But it is obviously much more difficult to achieve good results in very large groups. Some of the main problems are:

- **Communication**
  The learners may not all be able to see or hear you well, and you may not be able to see or hear all the learners well.

- **Numbers**
  There are several problems here:
  – It is very hard to get to know all the learners and their names.
  – The learners get much less individual practice.
  – There are too many pairs or groups for you to monitor.
  – You cannot often give learners individual feedback on written work.

- **Co-operation**
  Large groups are most common in captive learner situations—schools and universities where the students are obliged to attend the English courses. This means you are always likely to have a fair number of people who simply do not want to be there, or to co-operate with you and the other more motivated learners.

There are no magic, guaranteed solutions. The best starting point is probably obtaining the learners' co-operation. If the learners are adolescents or adults, you can discuss the challenges and options they face in their L1. The basic options are everybody co-operating and achieving some worth-while objectives, or everybody wasting their time. If a majority chooses the first option, which they probably will if you present it attractively, there is pressure on the minority at least not to disrupt the lessons.

You then need to face the problem of numbers. One way of tackling this problem is to form teams of eight to ten learners who agree to help one another, if possible with one or two learners who know a bit more English than the others in each team. You can use these teams for groupwork and pairwork, the stronger learners helping the weaker ones—in fact monitoring for you. You can also get regular written work from teams instead of every learner. In that case, make sure different members of the teams write out the work on different occasions, and that all members check and sign each piece of work.

You may need to organize practice on military lines at first, with clear, highly structured activities. This means accuracy work and simple reading and writing rather than free oral fluency work. If you can get the learners and the teams to attend and respond like a well-trained orchestra, even lockstep, team, and individual repetition can be quite satisfying for everybody. You can then get teams to prepare more complex fluency activities, for example, dialogues, role-plays, talks, and present them at the front of the class.

Summary

In Chapter 8 we have considered the following points:

Long-term planning. The course syllabus may be a document or the contents section of a coursebook. It should be the basis for all planning, and establish the goals, content, and time-scale of the course. If it is not a 'spiral' syllabus, constantly reactivating previously introduced items and integrating new items into a growing repertoire of English, try to introduce some of this yourself. Syllabus units should indicate how elements of the syllabus can be grouped and how fast the course should move. You may have to be very organized, disciplined, and creative to cover just the essential content of the syllabus in the time available.

Short-term planning. Work plans usually cover a week. They should keep you on course towards the main goals of the syllabus, and help maintain a balance of activities over several lessons. Lesson planning is essential preparation for teaching. Even good experienced teachers plan and make a few notes. It avoids going mechanically through the book or improvising whole lessons. Decide where a specific lesson fits into a week's work plan, and establish specific objectives. Activities and materials should be appropriate for your specific group of learners as well as the course objectives. Most lessons should include a warm-up, a main activity or activities, and a wind-down. A spare activity is also useful in case the lesson goes faster than anticipated.

Class management. You must be able to get the learners' attention quickly when you need it, for example, when giving instructions or explanations. There are non-verbal ways of doing this which avoid ineffectual and irritating shouting. For activities to work well, instructions should be clear, but also check comprehension and demonstrate the activity if necessary. Pair and groupwork require careful monitoring too. Learner participation, especially voluntary participation, depends largely on interest, involvement, and encouragement. Both teachers and learners need to play varying roles. Discipline, the main preoccupation of some teachers of children and adolescents, is largely achieved through planning, interesting topics and activities, motivation, fairness, and respect. If discipline problems do occur, maintain fairness and respect even when giving a punishment.

Different teaching situations. Two common teaching situations are working with children and working with large groups. Young children require lessons with a variety of concrete tasks (for example, moving around, doing things, repeating their favourite songs), frequent changes of activity, and an affectionate atmosphere. There are no magic, guaranteed solutions to the problems of large groups. However, it is vital to get co-operation from the majority of the group. It is also useful to form teams, with the stronger learners functioning as monitors. You need to adjust the course objectives to the reality of the situation, but it is usually possible to achieve worthwhile results.

Project

Giving instructions

Purpose: to develop the ability to give effective instructions.

Procedure:

1 Select a widely-used coursebook, and then a useful oral fluency activity in the book.
2 Analyse what exactly the learners have to do in the activity.
3 Write a full set of instructions for the activity, with a comprehension check. Include space for a demonstration if appropriate.
4 Record yourself giving the instructions, and consider how clear and effective they would be in a classroom.

9 WORKING WITH A COURSEBOOK

Introduction

In this chapter we look at how to use a coursebook, and what coursebooks can and cannot offer you. To use a coursebook well, you must know it well. You must also do much more than just work through the material and activities. You should plan lessons with your learners in mind, adapting and supplementing the book as appropriate. Finally, we consider criteria for choosing a coursebook.

Ways of using a coursebook

Most teachers use a coursebook, but in different ways. The factors affecting how teachers see and use a coursebook include:

- *Experience and training.* More experience and training usually mean less dependence on the book.
- *Workload.* Teachers with a heavy schedule and a variety of levels tend to depend on the book more than those with a light schedule.
- *Institutional policy.* Teachers tend to use a book more when supervisors insist on it and tests are closely based on it.
- *The quality of the coursebook.* Teachers naturally tend to use a book they like more than one they do not.

An inexperienced, untrained teacher with thirty hours of classes a week at different levels, in a school that emphasizes the use of the book, may use it eighty per cent of the time or more. An experienced, highly trained teacher with fifteen hours of classes a week, in a school that encourages teacher creativity, may use the book forty per cent of the time or less.

There are three common ways teachers actually use coursebooks:

1 As the course. The coursebook provides the course syllabus, virtually all the teaching–learning material and activities, and their sequence, and it determines the methodology. It establishes what to teach, when, and how. In effect, it is the course.

2 As the syllabus and main source of material. The coursebook provides the syllabus and many teaching–learning activities, and it influences the methodology. But teachers adapt and complement it. They omit some material and activities, using their own instead. Using the book as a basis, they produce a course they consider more suitable for their specific learners and teaching context, as well as their own personality and teaching style.

3 As one small element in the course. The other elements may be provided by the institution, for example, supplementary books or materials, videos, special classroom activities, and tests. Or they may be provided by individual teachers, for example, their own repertoire of materials, activities, and teaching strategies. The coursebook may be used mainly for homework and home study. This approach requires a high level of teacher organization.

For many teachers, especially those who start without practical training, these three ways of using a coursebook represent three stages of development. Better teaching is likely to result from the second and third approaches. The third approach especially requires considerable lesson preparation time and teacher creativity.

What coursebooks can offer

The syllabus

The table of contents, coursebook material, and Teacher's Guide can offer a clear programme of work, in other words, what to teach and in what order. The contents may consist of much more than a list of grammatical structures, functions, and vocabulary. They usually include communication situations and topics, and establish the balance between language work and skills work. The coursebook syllabus may even indicate how much time to spend on each unit.

Look at the table of contents of a beginners' coursebook.

BOOK 1   CONTENTS

Unit	Topics/functions	Language	Skills
1	**Hotel reception** • Greetings • Names • Requests • Identification of things • Numbers 1–10	• *Good morning/afternoon/ evening.* • *My name's _____ ./What's your name?* • *A single room, please./Here you are./Thank you.* • *What's this?/It's a key card.* • *One, two, three, etc.*	*Listening* • Hotel check-in *Speaking* • Hotel check-in
2	**Snack bar** • Introductions • Requests (cont.) • Identification (cont.) • Numbers 11–20	• *Hello. I'm _____ ./Pleased to meet you.* • *The menu, please.* • *What's number 15?/It's an ice-cream./Is number 6 a lemonade?/Yes, it is./No, it isn't.* • *Eleven, twelve, thirteen, etc.*	*Speaking* • Ordering in a cafeteria *Reading* • Australia
3	**Two towns** • Identification (cont.) • Location • Directions • Numbers 21–100	• *The White Horse is a hotel.* • *The post office is in Radford, near the bank.* • *Excuse me. Where's the station?/It's _____ .* • *Twenty-one, twenty-two, twenty-three, etc.*	*Listening* • Radio announcement *Speaking* • Buying a bus ticket • Information gap: Hotel

Review Unit

Unit	Topics/functions	Language	Skills
4	**Clothes shop/ Entertainments guide** • Price • Place • Time	• *The umbrella is $8./How much is that?* • *The Phantom of the Opera is at the Lyceum Theatre.* • *'Cats' is at 8 o'clock.*	*Speaking* • Asking directions *Reading* • Places in London *Writing* • Two cities

Questions

Could you put this syllabus into practice using your own materials and activities?
Would you need to see the material in the book to be confident about what to do?
Do you feel you would need to consult the Teacher's Guide to be really sure?

As a syllabus outline, a table of contents can be a practical starting point for a teacher's unit and lesson planning. It can help keep all the teachers in an institution working to similar plans, in similar ways. It can help institutions to co-ordinate and monitor teaching, and to prepare tests. It can also be useful to learners as a revision checklist, and as an indication of the objectives for the whole course. The information it provides allows learners to take more responsibility for their own learning, and casts light on the course they are taking rather than leaving them in the dark.

Language presentation material

Language presentation material may include visuals, printed models of language, and recorded models on audio-cassette or even video-cassette. Nowadays, coursebook presentation material usually attempts to provide a realistic context of use for the new language items.

If you use coursebook presentation material in class, you have to exploit it effectively for it to work. This is often best done with the learners' copies of the book closed. It is usually more motivating if you can bring material to life, not just leave it as texts and pictures on a page. You also need to make sure that the learners really notice the key features of the forms and structures and understand their meanings and functions. The presentation material in the coursebook is particularly useful for learners after class. It provides examples and a record of what they did in class, even if they did not actually use the book at the time. Studying examples at home, they may grasp things they missed in class. And if there is a learner's cassette, they can work on pronunciation at home.

Language practice material

Language practice material usually includes both oral and written activities. There should be fluency as well as accuracy work. Different interactions may be indicated, for example, lockstep, pair, group, or individual work.

Like presentation material, coursebook practice material can be useful, especially for inexperienced and hard-working teachers. But again, you have to exploit it effectively. Without appropriate handling, oral practice working from the book can become mechanical and boring for the learners. Like presentation material, practice material in the coursebook provides examples and a record of what learners did in class, and the opportunity to study at home.

Skills development material

Skills development material addresses the major objective of English teaching: enabling the learners to use the English language for real communication outside the classroom. Remember that all skills, receptive as well as productive, require the active involvement of the learners. The book alone cannot usually create this involvement.

The listening element may consist of verbal and perhaps visual material in the book, and a spoken text on an audio-cassette. You need to decide how exactly you are going to use the spoken text and any material in the book. You need to have a clear plan for carrying out a sequence of activities. If the spoken text is also printed in the book, one decision is whether or not to allow the learners to have their books open and read it as they listen. The listening and the reading material is likely to present you with other decisions too, for example:

– How to exploit the illustrations.
– How to handle the pre-listening and pre-reading stage.
– How to make the texts and tasks fully relevant to the learners' interests and needs.
– How to make the texts and tasks as appropriate as possible for the learners' abilities.

The speaking material will almost certainly require a lot of careful management and handling on your part. Again, a basic decision may be whether to work with books open or closed. Generally it is better to have books closed for communicative speaking activities. Then you may need to:

– Adapt activities to the learners' interests and needs.
– Bring situations to life, perhaps with specific aids or supplementary material.
– Explain and demonstrate activities and tasks.
– Organize changes of interaction, for example, lockstep to groupwork and back to lockstep.
– Monitor and help the learners during pair and groupwork.

The writing activities may require similar organizing and facilitating, though they tend to be less dynamic and demanding. It is often a good idea to have a quiet period of writing after oral work.

Coursebook skills development material can be useful for all teachers, but especially inexperienced and busy ones. It can be difficult, time-consuming, and costly to find or produce most of the material yourself, especially for listening and reading. But it is good if you can provide some material and activities with your own learners' interests and needs in mind.

A sequence of work

Presentation of new language items, then practice of new language items, then skills development is the sequence followed by units in most coursebooks. But even at beginner level, the coursebook authors may not design every lesson to begin with presentation and practice of new language items. The Teacher's Guide may recommend communicative warm-ups and extended communicative handling of presentation and practice topics or situations before you go into explicit presentation and practice work. In other words, the authors may intend that communication should be the base you constantly work from and return to.

What can be put into a coursebook is obviously limited, and you must handle the material in the light of recommendations in the Teacher's Guide and the principles in your own head that guide your teaching.

Recycling and review of language

It is difficult for teachers to cover the necessary recycling and review of previously practised language as systematically as a good coursebook. Most books nowadays have specific review units, and constantly recycle previously presented language. This may be done largely by means of skills work, where 'old' language can be combined naturally with new. In this way, language review does not become a boring task for learners since they will be practising 'old' language with fresh topics and tasks.

Additional material

Coursebooks may also offer pronunciation material, grammar summaries, vocabulary lists, teacher's notes, supplementary material, and tests:

– *Pronunciation material* in international and some regional coursebooks may not be relevant to your learners' problems and focus instead on things that are no problem for them. For example, certain sounds in English are difficult for Poles but easy for Turks, and other sounds are easy for Indonesians but difficult for Japanese. Teachers with satisfactory pronunciation themselves and an awareness of their learners' typical difficulties can usually handle this area much better than the coursebook.

– *Grammar summaries* can help you to clarify points in class, and are useful for learners to study at home. But it is important to remember that looking at a grammar table does not mean learners will understand, retain, or be able to use the grammar it contains.

– *Teacher's notes* can be especially useful for inexperienced teachers. They sometimes also offer good alternative or additional ideas for presentation, practice, and skills work that help you work outside the coursebook itself.

– *Supplementary material* is usually welcomed by both teachers and learners. Different coursebooks offer different supplementary material, both lo-tech such as wall-charts and flash-cards, and medium or hi-tech such as audio- and video-cassettes (see Chapter 10). Workbooks can extend the main coursebook, which is primarily intended for teaching–learning situations: they provide extra individual practice, either in class or for homework.

– *Tests* provided with a coursebook usually reflect the general approach of the course. However, teaching situations vary enormously, and coursebook tests may need to be adapted to the specific needs of your learners (see Chapter 11).

What a coursebook cannot provide

Most coursebooks for adults, and some for children, are written for international distribution. The authors probably do not know your country or your language, let alone your teaching institution and learners. Even locally produced coursebooks are probably written by authors who do not know your specific school or learners. The book can provide you with all the useful resources mentioned above, but only you, the teacher, can respond fully to your specific teaching conditions and your specific learners' interests and personalities. Only you, the teacher, can bring coursebook material to life and make it work in your classroom. This usually means adapting and supplementing the book to some extent. And a coursebook cannot have a personal relationship with the learners. Only you, the teacher, can project enthusiasm, respond sensitively to learners, and make language learning a personal, enjoyable, and satisfying activity.

Preparing to use a new coursebook

Before using a new coursebook, you should learn your way around it, getting to know:

- the syllabus (objectives, content, sequence, lesson or unit divisions)
- the layout (typical organization of each lesson or unit, format and presentation of the main types of material, including activities and exercises)
- the proposed methodology and procedures (suggested use of the coursebook as indicated by the types of activity, instructions, and the Teacher's Book)
- the supplementary material (audio-cassettes, workbook, wall-charts, etc.).

If you invest time doing this before you use the coursebook, you will be able to handle it more efficiently, effectively, and confidently when you actually teach with it. You may also find that you can begin to plan some adaptation of the book to suit your learners and yourself better.

Take a critical approach to your coursebook, even if it looks very good on the surface. Ask yourself questions like these:

- Is the syllabus practical, and at the appropriate level for my learners?
- Do the lesson or unit divisions fit the number of lessons I have each week?
- Is there an appropriate balance between language and skills work?
- Is all the presentation and practice material clear and realistic?
- Are the contexts and topics all appropriate for my learners?
- Are the 'communicative' material and activities really communicative?
- Is the methodology suggested suitable for my learners, and for my style of teaching?

Questions like these will help you decide how much you can work straight from the book, and how much you need to modify, substitute, or omit. For example, if question tags are included in Book 1, you may decide to omit them or deal with them for recognition only, and leave production for a later stage. Or if the book seems weak on conversation activities, you may decide to add some on topics of particular interest to your learners. When thinking about your coursebook in this way, consider the points that have come up in previous chapters of this book. For example, you might find that the reading comprehension tasks do not match the recommendations in Chapter 5. Perhaps they have no pre-reading activities and very repetitive comprehension exercises. In that case you may decide to supplement and adapt them. Such modifications to the syllabus, the materials, and teaching strategies can make a significant difference to the success of a course based on a coursebook.

Before you teach your first lessons with a new book it is useful to consider how you will design your lesson plans around the material. What will you usually handle with the book open, or with the book closed? What will you usually omit, supplement, or substitute? What will you usually handle in class, or leave for homework? Your plans will vary from lesson to lesson, and change as you gain experience working with the book, but an initial general plan of action can give you a better start.

Exploiting a coursebook

You can use many ideas with the book itself closed, though some material will of course require the learners to have their books open, for example, reading comprehension or written exercises. But the more you do with the book closed, and the more you add your own ideas to those in the book, the better your learners will respond. They will see you as a real teacher, not as someone who just goes mechanically through the coursebook.

Using language presentation material

Some presentation material may require the learners to have their books open, but it can often be used with the book closed at first. Looking at illustrations in the coursebook and reading model sentences as well as listening to you can distract the learners' attention from the pronunciation, the key grammatical features, and the meaning of the language you are presenting. You can 'lose' the learners in their books, or have them 'watching tennis' (i.e. looking at you, then the book, then you, then the book, and so on). It is often better to present new language without using the book material or ideas at all. Instead, you can use contexts or topics that are especially interesting or familiar for your learners. Later you can turn to the book to consolidate the language already presented. In fact, presentation material can often be used as follow-up material. For example, a dialogue in the book and on the cassette can be used for listening comprehension after you have presented the new language using your own material.

Opposite is some coursebook presentation material on comparison with adjectives.

Happy Vacations at the Hotel of Your Choice

THE BAY MOTEL

Quality and Economy
'Everything you need, nothing you don't'

- 80 rooms with color TV
- Restaurant and bar
- 3 miles from downtown San Francisco
- Modern—opened 1995
- And—$29 single! $39 double!

The Welcome Inn

A tradition for wise travelers since 1932

- 54 rooms, color TV
- Heated swimming pool
- Restaurant, bar, room service
- In the heart of San Francisco!
- Fantastic rates: $35 1 person, $45 2 persons

Listen to the dialogue.

Bob Well, what do you think? The Bay Motel or the Welcome Inn?

Jane The Bay Motel's cheaper than the Welcome Inn.

Bob Yes, but the Welcome Inn's more central.

Jane Mm, and it's nicer. I love that old building.

Bob It really is more convenient than the Bay Motel.

Jane OK, the Welcome Inn it is, then.

Questions

If you had to use this coursebook material with adults, how would you handle it?

With a group of adolescents, would you use, modify, or substitute this material?

If you decided to substitute it, what topic or situation would you use?

Possible ways of handling this specific material include:

- Discussing local hotels before learners open their books.
- Discussing the illustrations and general information about the hotels before focusing on comparison.
- Playing the dialogue cassette and asking comprehension questions.

- Repeating the models from the dialogue, highlighting the comparative forms '-er' and 'more . . . than'.
- Asking learners to repeat the models chorally and individually.
- Checking understanding by asking 'yes–no' questions about local hotels (for example, 'Is the _____ hotel cheaper/more modern than the _____ hotel?').
- Eliciting adjectives describing the hotels and listing them on the board in two columns, one column taking the '-er' form and the other the 'more + adjective' form. You could then ask the learners which adjectives take which form, and why.

Using language practice material

It is your teaching, not the coursebook, that determines whether practice is effective and enjoyable for the learners. It is essential to bring the material and activities to life, or modify them to suit your class if necessary.

Here is some coursebook practice material for questions and answers in the Present Tense:

1(a) Listen to the dialogue and complete it with expressions from the box.

How much	How long	How far	What time

Travel Agent	Good morning, can I help you?
Customer	Good morning, 1. _____ does the Bath City tour leave?
Travel Agent	At 2:00 p.m.
Customer	And 2. _____ is Bath?
Travel Agent	Oh, it's only thirty miles away.
Customer	Really. 3. _____ does that take?
Travel Agent	About forty-five minutes
Customer	4. _____ does it cost?
Travel Agent	£15, that includes transport to Bath and a one-hour city tour.
Customer	That's fine, I'll take two tickets please.

1(b) Ask and answer questions about the Bath City Tour, using expressions from the box.

---

2   Complete the following dialogue about the Chester City Tour.

Travel Agent   Good morning, can I help you?
Customer   1. _____ ?
Travel Agent   At 4:00 p.m.
Customer   2. _____ ?
Travel Agent   Oh, it's only twenty miles away.
Customer   3. _____ ?
Travel Agent   About twenty-five minutes.
Customer   4. _____ ?
Travel Agent   £8. That includes transport to Chester and a 45-minute city tour.
Customer   That's fine. I'll have a ticket please.

3   Look at the following information.

	OXFORD CITY TOUR	CAMBRIDGE CITY TOUR
Leaves	10:00 a.m.	8:00 a.m.
Returns	6:00 p.m.	8:00 p.m.
Distance	45 miles	70 miles
Journey takes	1 hr. 20 mins.	3 hrs.
Cost	£12	£25
Includes	snack	lunch
	1 hour tour	1 hour 30 mins tour

Ask and answer questions about the tours. Use: 'What time . . . ?', 'How far . . . ?', 'How long . . . ?', and 'How much . . . ?'

Questions

How could you interest young adult learners in activity 1a, and prepare them for it?
How could you organize and develop activity 1b?
How could you organize and develop activity 2?
How could you organize and develop activity 3?
Would you introduce any extra activities or stages of practice?

For 1a, you could do some pre-listening work with books closed, eliciting a little of what learners know about historic cities in their own country, and perhaps even in England. You could establish the tourist agency situation by asking learners if they know what tourist agencies are, who visits them, and why. Perhaps you could ask learners to give an example of a local tourist agency. Then you could ask what kind of questions they would expect to hear in a tourist agency. This might produce some essential language, for example 'How much?' and 'What time?' It would not matter if some of the learners' responses were in their native language, or if they asked 'How do you say _____ in English?' You could provide the questions in English if necessary and even write them on the board. You could then get the learners to open their books, read the incomplete dialogue, and predict answers before they listen to the cassette. After listening, you could get them to check their answers in pairs.

For 1b, you could work with the whole class, with perhaps a pairwork follow-up, with the expressions written up on the board, and books closed. You might make sure all errors are corrected, but by the learners themselves.

Learners could do 2 individually, then, after checking the answers, act out the dialogue in pairs, first reading from the book, and then perhaps acting from memory, with their books closed.

For 3, you might need to demonstrate with a learner, then get a pair of learners to demonstrate before all the learners work in pairs. You would still probably make sure most errors were corrected by the learners themselves. Then you might get pairs to volunteer to act out a dialogue from memory at the front of the class. Then you could set up a freer travel agency simulation in pairs or groups.

Using skills development material

This kind of material may be thin and artificial in some books, and ample and natural in others. It may be restricted to language that has been recently presented and practised, or it may use a wider range of language, especially in reading. It may take a general approach to the skills, or focus on specific sub-skills such as reading strategies such as scanning and skimming (see Chapter 6). It may deal equally with all skills, or be stronger on some and weaker on others. And it may integrate skills or keep them separate. You need to be aware of all these aspects of coursebook material, and modify it when appropriate and possible.

When you examine coursebook skills development material, remember that content (the real information and real interest it contains), and the types of interaction (for example, exchanging information and opinions) are at least as important as language. Remember also that you must bring the material to life for the learners, and that skills work should be enjoyable and satisfying.

Here is some coursebook reading comprehension material:

A **Write down three things you know about snakes.**

1 _____

2 _____

3 _____

B **Read the statements below. Then read the article and circle 'true' or 'false'.**

1	All snakes are poisonous.	true	false
2	Snakes have dry skin.	true	false
3	Snakes can hear.	true	false
4	Snakes are all slow.	true	false
5	Snakes cannot live in very cold climates.	true	false

The truth about snakes

The picture shows a rattlesnake attacking a victim. Rattlesnakes inject poison into the animals they bite. Many people believe all snakes do the same, but the truth is only a few snakes are poisonous. In fact, most people believe a lot of false information about snakes. For instance, snakes have dry, not wet skin. They cannot hear sounds, but they can feel vibrations. Snakes can move very fast: the black mamba can move at 11 kilometres per hour. Not all snakes are legless: some boas and pythons have very small legs. Some snakes do not lay eggs, but have live young. Not all snakes live in the tropics: the adder can live north of the Arctic Circle. Finally, not all snakes live on land; there are also fresh water and sea snakes.

C **Read the article again and answer these questions:**

1 How do rattlesnakes kill their victims?
2 What are some of the false ideas people have about snakes?
3 How do snakes perceive 'sounds'?
4 Which snakes have legs?
5 How are baby snakes born, from eggs or live from the mother snake?

D **Write down three things you have learnt about snakes.**

E **In pairs, discuss what you like or dislike about snakes and why.**

This material may seem very complete. The topic has potential interest for most people. It has a pre-reading activity (A). There is an illustration. There are two types of comprehension questions: true–false (B), and information questions (C). Learners are reminded of what they have learnt from reading (D). And there is a post-reading discussion activity, (E). One thing the material does not include is an explicit reading strategies component, though B is actually a scanning task. There is a little integration of skills in the above material: it is mainly a reading activity, but there is some writing and speaking, and consequently listening.

Questions

How could you maximize learner interest in the topic?
Would it be best to do A with books open or closed?
How could you exploit the illustration?
Should the learners do A, B, C, and D individually, or some sections in pairs or groups?
Should you give the learners the same time for C as for B?
What would you ask learners to do after D?
How would you check and correct each activity?

You could arouse learner interest by bringing a toy snake to class—there are some quite lifelike examples readily available! Let the learners handle it and then ask them whether they enjoyed it or not. Alternatively, you could ask the learners to name as many types of snake as possible and write up their suggestions on the board. Once you have a good number, ask the learners about the differences between them, for example, size and colour. Then ask them about the common characteristics of snakes and write up a list of these.

The pre-reading activity would probably best be done with books closed, but pre-reading could be continued by discussing the illustration in the book. It would be good to do B with a short time limit, say two minutes, to encourage fast scanning, but more time could be given for C. It might be a good idea to get learners to do C in pairs. Learners could discuss what they have written after D.

You could check answers with the whole class after each activity. With activity A, you could ask learners for their answers and write them up on the board without questioning their accuracy. Once the learners have read the text, you could go back to the list on the board and correct it. With B and C you can ask individual learners to give their answers and then check them with the rest of the class before writing up a correct set of answers on the board. Alternatively, you could ask learners to discuss their answers in groups and arrive at an agreed set of replies. Then you could ask each group to give their answers and check them with the other groups before writing them up on the board. With D and E there are no correct answers, but there might be ideas and opinions expressed by a majority of the class which can be written up and discussed. It is important that both you and the class respect dissenting opinions.

Using review and clarification material

Review material varies a great deal from book to book. The most important thing to remember is not to handle it just like presentation and practice activities. Learners should be able to work faster and more independently, with just a little assistance from you when absolutely necessary. It is your opportunity to observe how well they do, and to evaluate their progress. Of course, if you do note serious problems, you should do some remedial work, perhaps in the following lesson.

Lesson planning around coursebook material

Even with a coursebook, planning is important. It can help you:

- avoid potential problems in the material
- exploit strengths, and convert the material into lively classroom activities
- adapt the material to your learners' interests and needs, and to your own teaching style.

Plans based on coursebooks may be quite simple. Essentially, you need to note:

- the objectives and teaching points of the lesson
- the coursebook material and activities you will use
- the modifications you will make (different sequences, variations in exploitation)
- the supplementary material and equipment you will need
- the classroom management and interactions for each activity
- the approximate time for each activity.

A coursebook-based plan could look something like the one opposite.

Questions

Can you follow this plan, even without the actual material to be used?
Would this kind of plan suit you?
Would you modify anything in the format or the actual plan?

Group: 2A
Room: 16
Unit: 11
Time: 10.45–11.45
Date: 20th May

Objectives/teaching points: Presentation /Practice of comparison (add 'more' to '-er').
Development of conversation and listening skills.

Specific objectives/ activities	Materials/aids	Procedures/ interactions	Time
1 Warm-up: animal topic (*-er*)	Photos of pets	T on pets → TQ–LA → TQ–LA → threes	5'
2 Comparison: dogs (*more*)	Cut-outs on board	T model → elicit → drill → PRS	15'
3 Comparison: wild animals (*more* and *-er*)	Book p.37, A	TQ–LA on pics → T–L demo → L–L demo → PRS → check	10'
4 Written exercise	Book p.37, B	IND → PRS check → class	10'
5 Pre-listening: robots	Flashcards on board	TQ–LA → GPS decide on work of each robot → check	5'
6 Listening: robots	Book/cass. p. 38, D	Book tasks, (b) in PRS	10'
7 Extra: robots vs. humans	Open discussion	Class → GPS → class	?

Notes: Sandra coming to visit class!
Homework: Book p. 39, E.

Key: T = teacher; TQ = teacher questions; L = learner; LA learner answers; PRS = pairs; GPS = groups; IND = individual; → = leads to/followed by

Choosing a coursebook

Most teachers use coursebooks chosen by other people, for example, the co-ordinator or principal of the school where they work. However, it is important to understand what is involved in choosing a coursebook so that you can analyse and evaluate your particular book and see its strengths and weaknesses. Also, you may at some time be involved in the selection process yourself.

Here are four key questions to ask yourself about your coursebook:

- *Is it right for your institution?* Consider points like:
    - compatibility with the official syllabus
    - compatibility with your institution's English teaching objectives and general curriculum
    - suitability for the teaching–learning conditions, for example, group size, course hours.

- *Does it suit your experience and the way you teach?* Consider points like:
    - your level of experience and training
    - your proficiency in English
    - cultural and personal factors, for example, your interests, your gender.

- *Is it right for your learners?* Consider points like:
    - their age, education, gender, interests, and needs
    - their motivation and attitude towards the English language and the related culture
    - the price—can they afford it?

- *Is it right as a coursebook?* Consider points like:
    - the syllabus design, for example, language content, organization, skills content
    - the materials and activities for presentation, practice, skills, review
    - the physical presentation, for example, layout, visuals, durability
    - support materials, for example, cassettes, teacher's book
    - value for money and availability.

The evaluation of a coursebook before actually using it is usually unreliable. If you know teachers who are already using a book you are interested in, ask them what they think of it. See if it is possible to pilot the book before you take a final decision. Ultimately there is only one way to evaluate a coursebook—by actually using it over a period of time. You may have doubts about a book at first, and grow to like it later, or like a book at first, and grow to have reservations about it later. Remember that no book is perfect in itself, or for a particular teaching–learning context. In the final analysis, you have to make a coursebook work. That usually means adapting and supp-lementing it in some way for your own specific learners and teaching context.

Summary

In Chapter 9 we have considered the following points:

Ways of using a coursebook. A coursebook can be used as the course, as the basis for the course, or mostly for homework and home study. It is natural for teachers with little experience and heavy workloads to rely on the book a good deal. But as they acquire experience and training, and encounter better teaching conditions, most teachers begin to adapt and supplement their coursebooks creatively.

What coursebooks can offer. The syllabus can give teachers and the learners a clear programme of work. Presentation of new language items, followed by practice and skills development is the sequence followed by most coursebook units, although there may be additional communicative work. Recycling and reviewing language can be done much more systematically in coursebooks than by individual teachers. Grammar summaries, vocabulary lists, the Teacher's Guide, supplementary material, and tests can all be useful. A coursebook can be a vital aid and resource for your teaching, but it cannot be perfect for your specific learners, teach itself, or provide your human touch.

Preparing to use a new coursebook. Before using a new coursebook in class it is important to become familiar with its main components and features. You will then be able to use it effectively and confidently, and even adapt it to suit your learners and yourself better. Lesson planning is particularly important when using a new book.

Exploiting a coursebook. Teachers need strategies for working with the book open and closed. It is generally best to have it closed as much as possible, even when using coursebook ideas. Teachers also need specific strategies for handling coursebook presentation material, practice material, and skills development material. The principles and techniques for these stages or areas of teaching are essentially those discussed in the relevant chapters of this book. Teachers also have to bring coursebook material to life and convert it into effective, enjoyable classroom activities. Without the appropriate dynamics, working from the book can become mechanical and boring for the learners.

Lesson planning around coursebook material. Apart from the usual advantages of lesson planning, when you are working with a coursebook, planning can help you avoid weaknesses in the material, convert it into lively classroom activities, and adapt it to your learners' interests and needs. Planning can also help you to integrate book material with other appropriate material and ideas.

Choosing a coursebook. You should consider whether a coursebook is right for your institution, for the way you teach, for the learners, and as a coursebook. However, the only way to really evaluate a coursebook is by using it over a period of time. Even then, a coursebook is really only as good as the teacher who uses it.

Project

Coursebook analysis and lesson planning

Purpose: to develop the ability to use a coursebook effectively.

Procedure:

1 Select a widely-used coursebook, and then a lesson or unit from the middle of the book.
2 Analyse the objectives, and the material and activities in the selected lesson or unit.
3 Check what functions, structures, and vocabulary have been covered in all the previous lessons or units.
4 Write a lesson plan for a sixty-minute class using materials and/or activities from the selected lesson or unit combined with materials and/or activities you find elsewhere or create yourself. Pay attention to class management, including when you work with the book open and with the book closed.

10 TEACHING AIDS AND MATERIALS

Introduction

In this chapter we look at the use of aids and materials in different teaching contexts. Effective use of the most basic piece of classroom equipment, the board, requires organizational skills as well as adequate writing and drawing. Board drawings can be supplemented by other visual material, and by real objects and mime. We extend the discussion of audio-cassettes in Chapter 5, particularly with respect to songs. The effective use of video requires much thought and planning, but the range of possible uses is greater than most people realize.

Different teaching contexts

The contexts in which English is taught vary greatly. In some institutions the classrooms have framed posters on the walls. There is a cabinet at the front containing video equipment and an audio-cassette player. The learners all have a copy of the attractive coursebook. And there is a teachers' resource centre with a wide range of supplementary materials. In other institutions, the classroom walls are bare. There is nothing but chairs, a table, and a board. And the learners, or most of them, do not have books.

In spite of the great differences in resources, the teachers in both the above situations can give effective classes. And they need to be equally creative, skilled, and organized. If they are not, they will fail to engage the learners in effective learning, even if they have access to the most sophisticated resources.

Using the board

The board is usually the most basic piece of classroom equipment. A lot can be done with it if you know how: for instance, writing up examples and exercises, or supporting your teaching with diagrams, tables, and drawings.

Writing and general organization

Writing is a very personal matter—we identify ourselves with our handwriting. But your writing on paper does not necessarily transfer well to the board. Sometimes you need to make a real effort to change the way you write on the board. Some of the samples of board writing in Figure 10.1 are obviously much easier to read, and therefore better models to follow, than others.

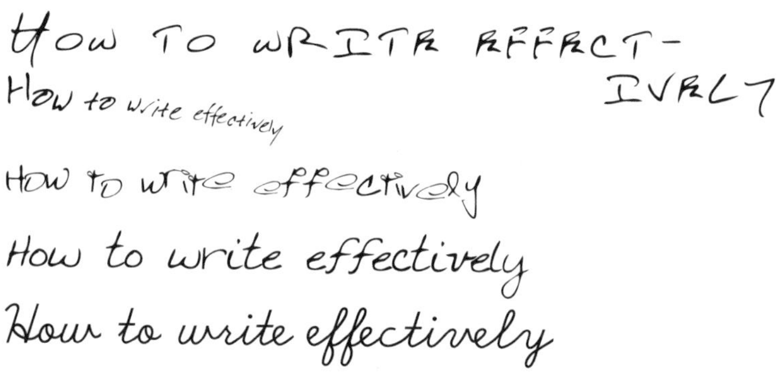

Figure 10.1: Handwriting of varying degrees of clarity

Clear writing on the board is also a matter of organization and good habits. It is easy to decide which of the boards in Figure 10.2 is better organized and clearer for the learners.

There are several simple lessons to learn from these two examples:

– Put things you want to leave on the board in an organized way at one side.
– Erase things you no longer need before writing anything else important.
– Write exercises and other things you want learners to copy in a clear space where nothing else interferes or distracts.

During a lesson, check the board periodically to see if it is clear and organized, if it has things on it that should be erased, or if it is time to clean it completely. Incidentally, it is a good habit to clean the board at the end of every class, ready for your next class or the next teacher.

Thursday, March 1st

rice

diamonds   Name: ....

sheep

            1. Where...... rice.......?

grown   It...... ...... in the south.

mined   2. Where...... diamonds.........?

reared   They..... ...... in the north.

            3. Where...... sheep.......?

                  .... in the west.

Thursday, March 1st

    Made in Japan/manufactured by......

                  1. Where...... rice......?

...... is/are......ed/n (Passive Voi   It...... .... in the

south.

rice   nort 2. Where...... diamonds......?

grown, reared   west + They...... ...... in the north.

sheep   sout 3. Where...... sheep......?

diamonds...... mined (coal, iro   .... in the

west.

    Don't forget your name at the top!

Figure 10.2: Good and poor board layouts

Board drawing

Combined with real objects, gesture, or mime, board drawings can avoid a lot of lengthy explanation in the learners' L1, or translation. Here are some examples of simple drawings that convey clear concepts visually.

These drawings are based on very simple elements and principles:

- Circles or ovals plus a few lines and dots for mouth, eyes, and eyebrows, representing facial expressions.
- Lines for the positions of body, arms, and legs, with a circle for the head ('stick figures') representing human activities. A little background (for example, the cliff for 'climbing') is sometimes necessary or useful.
- Simple line representations of common objects or places (for example, cage, bird).

Almost anyone can do a little simple drawing. In fact it is better if your drawings are 'as simple as a child's'. That way they usually function as recognizable symbols and can be done quickly. Detailed drawings are often not so clear as conventional symbols, and usually take a long time to do. You can build up whole scenes. Opposite is an example.

This drawing could be used for language practice, for example:

Learner A   You can climb in the park.
Learner B   Yes, two men are climbing the cliff. You can swim in the park.
Learner A   Yes, three children are swimming in the lake. You can . . .

It could also be used as a basis for written compositions.

An important point to remember when building up a scene, or sequence of drawings, is that you cannot expect the learners to wait patiently for several minutes while you do the drawing. You should do one of these three things:

– Do the drawing before the class begins.
– Give the learners something to do while you are drawing (for example, a pair or group oral activity or short written exercise).
– Ask the learners questions as you draw, for example, 'What do you think this is?'; 'Are these people adults or children?'; 'A horse, right. Can you ride a horse, Silvia?'

Remember also that the same principles of general organization and 'good habits' apply to drawing as to writing on the board.

Designing and using prepared visual materials

Teachers who are not confident about drawing on the board may prefer to use visual materials which have been prepared before the class. These can be made at home using pictures cut out of magazines, perhaps combined with drawing or writing. Some prepared visual materials, such as wall-charts and cue-cards, are useful for all teachers, even if they are good at drawing on the board.

Wall-charts

Some coursebooks provide ready-made posters or wall-charts, but you can also make your own at home. They can be scenes, like the national park drawing on page 157, or separate but related pictures, as in the example below.

One use of wall-charts is for lockstep work on new functional-grammatical items. This one could be used for work on 'too' and 'enough'. Another use is for vocabulary or conversation work. With this one you could elicit from the learners the words for all the parts of the cars, for example, 'wheel', 'tyre', and 'windscreen'. Or the learners could discuss which car they would like and why, for example:

Learner A   I'd like the Panther. It looks so impressive.
Learner B   I wouldn't spend £15,000 on a car! I'd like the . . .

Wall-charts need to be clear for all the learners, including those at the back of the room or to one side. This means that you need to select cut-out pictures which are large enough, and with strong outlines or contrasting tones, not all dark or all light tones. Any writing on the wall-chart also needs to be large enough and in a strong colour or dark tone.

Cue-cards

Like wall-charts, these need to have clear pictures and writing. They are easiest to handle if they are about twenty-five centimetres square and on stiff card, not floppy paper. It also helps to keep them in good condition if you cover them with transparent adhesive plastic, preferably non-reflecting. They may have words, simple drawings, or magazine pictures on them as in the examples below.

You could use any of these types of cue-card to elicit 'I like/don't like cats/dogs/parrots/fish' by showing a card to the class and then nominating a learner to respond. They can also be stuck on the board to remind learners of the different questions they can ask in pair or groupwork, for example, 'Have you got a _____ ?'

Real and imaginary objects

Drawings and other visual aids bring representations of real things into the classroom. But you can actually bring a wide variety of real things (*realia*) into the classroom. Alternatively, you can create objects and events in the learners' imaginations through mime.

Realia

Pens, pencils, books, desks, chairs and other typical classroom objects have probably always been used—and often boringly over-used—by language teachers for items like 'This is my chair'; 'What colour is your pen?', and 'I've got two pencils'. But there are many other, potentially more interesting, objects that can be used in the presentation and practice of language.

Teaching ideas

- You can use your own and the learners' possessions, for example, keys, watches, and calculators. You will find this kind of realia in some of the earlier chapters, for example, in Chapter 3, Extract 7, for practice of 'My _____ was made in _____ '. They could also be used for practising language such as 'This is . . . '; 'What colour . . . ?'; 'I've got . . . '; possessives ('Whose sweater is this?'), and for materials things are made of ('My sweater is made of wool').

- Possessions can also be used for vocabulary revision or extension. For example, you and the students put a variety of possessions on the desk at the front of the class, then teams write a list of all the things they can name. The team with the most correct items wins. The learners can discover new vocabulary from one another in the process.

  If the words for all objects should be known to the learners, you can organize a memory game. After the learners have looked at the objects on the desk for a minute or two, cover them with a cloth, and then get the learners to say or write on the board all the objects they can remember.

- Specific realia can be used to illustrate stories, especially with children. For example, a story about the jungle is much more attractive for them if they have toy animals to look at and even touch. You cannot take real monkeys and lions to class, but you can take real toys.

Mime and gesture

Instead of using realia, you can create objects and events in the imagination of the learners with mime.

Teaching ideas

- Mime actions and get the learners to respond, for example, 'You're eating a banana/ice-cream' (Present Progressive + vocabulary) or 'You've combed your hair/put on a hat' (Present Perfect + vocabulary). Give cards with actions written on them to learners (for example, 'driving a car' or 'reading a newspaper'). Get learners to mime the action in front of the class for the other learners to guess.

- Mime and gesture can also be used for listening comprehension and vocabulary work (see Chapter 4), page 67. Select or write a story, decide which words you can leave out, and tell the story pretending you cannot think of those words. When you reach one of the words, mime them instead and get the learners to provide the missing vocabulary.

Audio-cassettes

We considered the importance of audio-cassettes in teaching the spoken language in Chapter 5. We will look here at some other considerations and uses.

Materials and activities

The most common source of audio-cassette texts is the coursebook. It is important that these recordings are clear, at an appropriate speed for the learners (natural, but not too fast), and realistic, preparing the learners for listening outside the classroom. Coursebook recordings can also provide models for pronunciation and guided conversation work.

You can supplement your coursebook cassettes with other material specially selected for your own learners. Some of it may be authentic, in the sense that it was not designed for learners of English. It can include excerpts from the radio (for example, the news for adult learners), stories (for example, cassette versions of children's or adults' books, which are now widely available), and pop songs, which are particularly attractive for teenagers. If you think a text would really interest your learners, but it is a little above their level, you can often still use it successfully with a simple listening task. There is a useful principle that applies to both listening and reading comprehension: if the text is above the learners' level, make the task simple; if the text is below their level, make the task more complex. You can also divide a long text into sections, each with its separate task, in order to facilitate comprehension.

Teaching ideas

Here are some ideas specifically for handling songs.

- **Selecting and introducing songs**

  Select a song suitable for the learners and your teaching objectives. It should be attractive as well as appropriate for the level of the class. If you want to do language work, it should, of course, contain examples of the structures, functions, or vocabulary you want to work on. If you want to do comprehension or discussion work, the lyrics should convey interesting ideas or a story. If you are using a popular song by a well-known singer, play the beginning of the song and see if the learners can name the song and the singer. Ask them what they know and think of the singer. This can be done in lockstep or in groups.

- **Ordering phrases**

  Write phrases from the song on the board in scrambled order. Add spaces for numbers. The examples below are from the Irish folk-song 'Cockles and mussels'.

  a she caught a fever _____
  b girls are so pretty _____
  c her ghost wheels the barrow _____
  d she wheeled her wheelbarrow _____

  Check the learners' comprehension of the phrases. Then tell them to listen to the song and number the phrases in the order in which they occur in the song. The answers here are: b–1, d–2, a–3, c–4 (see the song below).

- **Scrambled lyrics**

  Take several photocopies of the lyrics, cut them into single lines or pairs of lines, and put them into scrambled sets. Divide the class into groups of three to five and give each group a set. Tell the groups to put the lyrics into the correct order. Then play the song two or three times so that they can check and if necessary change the order they have.

- **Gapped lyrics**

  With correction fluid, white-out some words or phrases from the lyrics. Alternatively, type out the lyrics with gaps for some of the words or phrases, for example:

  Cockles and mussels

  In Dublin's fair _____ where girls are so _____ ,
  I first set my _____ on sweet Molly Malone,
  As she wheeled her wheelbarrow through _____ broad and narrow,
  _____ , 'Cockles and mussels, alive, alive, oh!'

  Alive, alive, oh! Alive, alive, oh! Crying, 'Cockles and mussels, alive, alive, oh!'

  She _____ a fever and no one could _____ her,
  And that was the _____ of sweet Molly Malone,
  But her _____ wheels the barrow through _____ broad and narrow,
  _____ , 'Cockles and mussels, alive, alive, oh!'

  Alive, alive, oh! Alive, alive, oh! Crying, 'Cockles and mussels, alive, alive, oh!'

(Missing words:
First verse: city, pretty, eyes, streets, crying
Second verse: caught, save, end, ghost, streets, crying)

Photocopy this 'gapped' version and distribute it to the learners. In pairs, they read it and complete what they can. Play the song so that the pairs can check or complete missing items. If the learners are having difficulty, write the missing words or phrases scrambled on the board and play the song once more.

- **Finding examples of a structure**

  If you have selected a song for language consolidation work, ask the learners to find examples of a particular structure.

  (Note that many of these ideas can be used with other listening texts as well as songs, for example, dialogues and radio or television news.)

Video

These days, there is an increasing amount of video material available. For example, most coursebooks now have their own video cassettes, and supplementary video material is produced by many ELT publishers. In addition, there is an enormous number of films and documentaries on sale to the general public. These usually cost much less than ELT material since they are sold to a much larger market. Then there are television programmes and commercials.

The effective use of video requires knowledge and planning. Video sessions can easily become lessons in which teachers switch the video on and themselves off. Instead of being fun and useful, they can be demotivating, frustrating, or boring for the learners. Simply switching the video on and letting, or making, the learners watch and listen is seldom either useful or enjoyable. Only a little of all the material available will be suitable for your learners and your teaching purposes. You should select material with clear objectives and the learners' level and interests in mind, and get to know it well before using it. There should be a clear purpose for every video clip you show, for example, modelling communicative interactions in English, working at language forms, developing listening comprehension, or generating discussion.

The integration of video into your lessons will depend on how access to video is organized where you teach. If there is a video player in each classroom, you can use it at any stage of any lesson, even for very brief periods. In contrast, if you have to reserve a video room, you may be able to use it only occasionally. You will then need to plan the sessions very carefully to take advantage of these opportunities.

Selecting material

Any videos accompanying your coursebook should be at an appropriate level of difficulty for the learners, and relevant to the course syllabus. Even so, you need to decide what you will use and what you will omit, just as with any other coursebook material (see Chapter 9). You need to think even more carefully about using supplementary video material. Non-ELT or 'authentic' material, for example, feature films or documentaries, television program-mes or commercials, requires much more time and care. You need to find extracts that suit your teaching objectives, and then design activities, and perhaps worksheets, for them. You should not use material simply because it is available, but because it really serves your purposes. Ask yourself these questions:

– Will the learners understand the material well enough, either because they are familiar with the language used, or because the visual element makes it fairly clear?
– Will the learners enjoy the material, because it is interesting, humorous, or relevant to their needs?
– Do I have some really useful activities with which to exploit the material?
– Is there any alternative way of achieving my teaching objectives more effectively or in less time than with video?

Teaching ideas

The activities you use to exploit video are usually at least as important as the material itself, often more important.

• The most obvious use of video is for listening comprehension. Show a short section of video, put it on pause, ask questions about what the people said, then show another section, and so on. You can also ask questions which are not about the script, but about the scene and what is happening.

Here are some ways of using video for giving models of language:

• Ask the learners to listen for a specific form or functional expression, for example, a conditional sentence, or an apology. Write an example of the form or function you want them to listen for on the board and get them to raise their hands when they hear one.

- Use the pause button to stop the video after selected forms or functional expressions, and ask the learners to repeat what the last speaker in the video said. This keeps the learners listening attentively, and focuses on the forms or expressions you have selected.

- Use the pause button to stop just before a speaker in the video says something you want to focus on, and ask the learners to predict what that speaker will say. Then start the video again so that the learners can compare what is said with what they predicted. This is particularly appropriate when the visual element of the video gives clear clues, and with routine interactions that follow a fairly predictable course, for example, checking in at the airport or shopping.

- Tell the learners to pay careful attention to a short sequence because you want volunteers to act out approximately what they hear and see afterwards. You may play the sequence two or three times. This is particularly suitable for practising the language of typical interactions, for example, giving street directions, or eating in a restaurant.

Here are some ways of using video for generating language use by the learners. All of these activities require some fluency in English, and are best used only with quite good elementary learners or with learners at intermediate level or above.

- Turn the contrast and brightness right down or cover the screen, so that the learners can hear but cannot see what is happening. Play a short section, preferably one with several background sounds and not much dialogue. Then get the learners to discuss in pairs or groups where the scene is and what is happening. Afterwards, play the section with both sound and vision so they can see whether they were right or not. A sequence with characteristic sounds is best, for example, a street, an office, or a factory.

- Show a short section of video with the sound off. Then get the learners, in pairs or groups, to discuss what they saw, what they think was happening, and what they think was said. This is often best done with fairly ambiguous sequences where different viewers may have different ideas which generate discussion. Then play the section with the sound turned up so that the pairs or groups can find out who got closest to the facts.

- Play a section of video on fast-forward so that it is like a speeded up silent movie. Then get the learners, in pairs or groups, to discuss what they think was happening. A section with a lot of action is best for this. It can be equally effective—and even more amusing—to use rewind instead of fast-forward.

- Get the learners to sit in pairs facing each other, so that one of them can see the video and the other cannot. The learner who can see describes to the other what is happening. After a while, stop the video and get them to change places. This activity can be very challenging, and a sequence that requires only simple vocabulary and grammar is essential for lower levels. It also helps if you use the pause button at regular intervals so that the learner describing the action can keep up. This activity is generally suitable only for learners at intermediate level or above.

Summary

In Chapter 10 we have considered the following points:

Different teaching contexts. Teaching contexts range from those in which there is video in every classroom and a teachers' resource centre, to others in which a board is the only equipment. But teachers in any situation need to be creative, skilled, and organized if they are to be effective.

Using the board. The board is the most universal and basic piece of classroom equipment. Your writing on the board should be clear, and your use of the board organized. Virtually any teacher can learn to do some simple drawing, which can help avoid the use of L1 and translation. Drawings can be used for a variety of purposes, including vocabulary work and guided composition.

Designing and using prepared visual materials. Wall-charts and cue-cards can be made from pictures cut out of magazines and other sources. Wall-charts can consist of scenes, or separate but related pictures. They can be used for work on new language items, and for conversation or guided composition work. Cue-cards can also be used for both lockstep and pair and groupwork.

Real and imaginary objects. Realia should be not restricted to such things as pens and books. The learners' own possessions can often be used, as well as things you take to class specially. Apart from using realia in the presentation and practice of new language items, you can use them in a variety of review, story-telling, and other activities. Mime and gesture can also be very useful and fun, creating objects and actions in the learners' imaginations.

Audio-cassettes. Audio-cassettes can bring realistic or authentic listening material into the classroom. The most obvious source of cassette texts is the coursebook, but other materials are not hard to find. These may include songs, which most learners like, and which can be handled in many useful and interesting ways.

Video. There is a wide variety of material available, from coursebook and other ELT videos to films and television. Your use of video will depend to some extent on whether you have it permanently available in your classroom or can use it only occasionally. In either case, you should consider carefully what your objectives are in using it, and not use it simply because it is available, perhaps wasting time and frustrating or boring the learners. Appropriate material and activities can be very useful and fun. Apart from listening comprehension work, video can be used in a variety of activities that either provide models of English in use, or generate discussion among the learners.

Project

Preparing and using listening materials

Purpose: to develop the ability to produce and evaluate listening materials.

Procedure:

1 Select a song in English that you:
    a   predict a specific group of learners you know will like.
    b   can use for either language or discussion work as well as comprehension work. Obviously, you must have the cassette of the song, and the lyrics.
2 Study the 'Teaching ideas' in the Audio-cassettes section again, and decide how you will prepare the learners for the song, which type of activities you will use with the song itself, and what follow-up activity you will use.
3 Prepare a teaching plan and the material for the activities planned.
4 If possible, use the plan and material with the learners you were thinking of.
5 If you are able to teach the plan, reflect afterwards on how it went, and what changes you would make if you were to use the song and activities again. If you are not able to teach the plan, leave it for a week without looking at it. Then go through the plan and material with the cassette, imagining any problems you might encounter and thinking how you could avoid them.

11 TESTING AND EVALUATION

Introduction

In this chapter we look at the connections and differences between teaching, testing, and evaluation. Different types of test are discussed, with a focus on achievement tests. The key principles of test writing, including validity and reliability, are explained. Finally, we consider how teaching, materials, and courses can be evaluated. All evaluation should be for the benefit of the learners.

Teaching, testing, and evaluation

No important enterprise should just go on and on without some kind of evaluation. Teaching and learning are no exception. A lot of thought and effort are usually put into testing 'the learners' or 'learning', but it is important to think beyond that.

Teaching and testing

There is an intimate relationship between teaching and testing, but they are not the same thing. Unfortunately, some teachers convert teaching into a kind of continuous test. For example, the following excerpt from a 'conversation' session:

Teacher	Where did you go in the holidays, Sofia?
Learner 1	I didn't go anywhere.
Teacher	Very good, very good. And you, Giovanni. Where did you go?
Learner 2	I go to Scotland.
Teacher	No, no, Giovanni, no.

This is a very strange conversation. The teacher seems to be happy that Sofia did not go anywhere in the holidays, and he does not seem to believe that Giovanni went to Scotland. Of course, what the teacher is doing is responding only to the *language* of the learners' replies, not the *information*. He indicates that Sofia's sentence is linguistically 'very good', but Giovanni's sentence is not. It is not real conversation practice at all.

Obviously, you do need to deal with errors like Giovanni's, but as much of your teaching as possible should be directed towards building up the learners' ability and confidence in using English for effective communication. Especially when you are trying to develop fluency, it is very important that the learners should not feel that they are being tested all the time. If they do, they will become more inhibited and never achieve fluency. Most teaching should not be testing, and should not be seen as a test by the learners. But you should be evaluating the learners' performance and progress—and your own teaching—constantly. Evaluation is essential in teaching.

Testing and evaluation

The two concepts *testing* and *evaluation* are expressed by the same word in many languages. However, the distinction that is conveyed by the two different words in English is important. Evaluation is a more general concept than testing. You can evaluate teaching, teaching materials, and even tests, as well as learning. Also, learning can be evaluated in several different ways, not only with the formal tests that you give the learners.

If the teacher of the 'conversation' session above had not focused exclusively on the language of the learners' replies, he might have been able to evaluate their progress much better:

Teacher	Where did you go in the holidays, Sofia?
Learner 1	I didn't go anywhere.
Teacher	You stayed here in Milan?
Learner 1	Yes, I just played with my friends.
Teacher	Well, that's always good fun. *[Teacher's evaluation: Sofia is doing very, very well!]* And you, Giovanni. Where did you go?
Learner 2	I go to Scotland.
Teacher	That's great! You went with your family, I suppose.
Learner 2	No, I go . . . I went with the family of a friend.
Teacher	I see. OK, everyone—ask Giovanni questions about his trip to Scotland.

[Teacher's evaluation: Giovanni understands very well, and gets his ideas across, but he is erratic with grammar. I must do some remedial work on the Past Tense.]

A test is normally carefully designed for a specific purpose, while some evaluation may be spontaneous and handled very flexibly. A test normally consists of one or more exercises or tasks, each with clear objectives. The evaluation of learning usually employs formal tests, but it may also include other options, one of which is demonstrated above. When the evaluation of learning is based on class participation, progress tests, homework, and projects rather than final tests alone, the term 'assessment' or 'continuous assessment' is often used.

However, tests continue to be the main instruments for evaluation of learning in most teaching situations. They are part of the reality of the classroom everywhere. For these reasons, this chapter focuses mainly on tests and testing.

Basic aspects of testing

Types of test

The purpose of English language tests is to gather reliable evidence of what learners can do in English and what they know of English. This information may be required for different reasons, and these reasons govern the type of test used. There are five common types of test, each with a specific purpose. These are shown in Table 11.1.

Table 11.1: The five common types of test and their purposes

Type of test	Purpose
Placement test	To place new students in the appropriate course or level. These are essential in large institutions that frequently receive new students.
Diagnostic test	To find out learners' strengths and weaknesses at the start of a course. They allow the teacher to adjust his or her teaching to the needs of the group and individual learners. They are especially useful with mixed-level groups.
Progress tests (short-term achievement tests)	To check how well learners are doing after each lesson or unit, and provide consolidation or remedial work if necessary. They usually focus on language that has recently been introduced and practised.

Course tests (longer-term achievement tests)	To check how well learners have done over a whole course. These are the commonest basis for the marks teachers give learners at the end of each course. They are very significant for learners. They are also the main concern in testing for most classroom teachers.
Proficiency tests	To determine learners' levels in relation to generally accepted standards. These are useful for the objective evaluation of learning, and also for the indirect evaluation of course design and teaching. The two best known systems of international proficiency tests are the UCLES exams and the TOEFL tests.

Validity and reliability

Professional test development and management is a highly complex matter. Anyone who is involved in the preparation of important tests should have some basic understanding of two concepts, *validity* and *reliability*, and the relationship between them.

An achievement test can be considered to have validity if:

– it contains only forms and uses the learners have practised in the course
– it employs only exercises and tasks that correspond to the general objectives and methodology of the course.

The first type of validity, called *content validity*, means that the grammar, vocabulary, and functional content of a test should be carefully selected on the basis of the course syllabus. This is only logical and fair. If the learners have not practised the Passive Voice, they should not be tested on it. If they have not practised the vocabulary of cooking, they should not be tested on it. The language content of the test should go outside the syllabus only when it is not significant in the exercise or task: for example, in a reading comprehension test, where the learners may actually have been encouraged to ignore incidental language they do not know or to guess its meaning from context. The second type of validity, called *construct validity*, means that the exercises and tasks in a test should be similar to those used in the course and correspond to the general approach of the course. If the learners have never practised translating on the course, they should not have to translate a passage in the test. If the main aim of the course has clearly been to use grammar in natural discourse such as conversations, the grammar should not be tested only through grammar manipulation exercises. If a test conforms to these principles, it will probably be seen as fair by the teachers and the learners. If it does not, it will probably be considered unfair, and justifiably so.

Reliability is a matter of how far we can believe or trust the results of a test. For example, you may question the reliability of a test when two of your own groups that you consider very similar in ability and achievement get very different results in the same test, one group doing well and the other badly.

A specific test exercise or task is normally reliable when:

- the instructions are clear and unambiguous for all the learners
- the exercise or task controls to some extent how learners respond, for example, it should be clear in 'fill the gap' exercises whether a single word or a phrase is required
- there are no errors in the test, for example, if the learners have to 'select the best answer—a, b, c, or d', there should not actually be two or more acceptable answers.

The reliability of a test also depends partly on how far it can be marked objectively. Multiple choice exercises, where the learner has to select the best answer from a choice of three or four, are purely objective by nature. One-word fill-in exercises—completion of a text with one word in each space—are purely objective when only one word is possible. But when many different words are possible, they are fairly subjective, requiring teachers to use their personal judgement. Composition marking is by nature highly subjective.

The reliability of a test also depends on its length and on how it is administered. A long test is usually more reliable than a short one. Any test provides a sample of a learner's English, and a small sample of something is less reliable than a large one.

The administration of a test may affect its reliability. For example, reliability is reduced if:

- one group is given much more time than another
- one group is helped by the teacher and another is not
- invigilation is strict in one group and not in another, so that there is a lot of copying or other types of cheating in the second group.

Balancing validity and reliability

A valid test for a course with communicative objectives should include exercises and tasks in which the learners use language in realistic contexts. For example, they could complete a dialogue, write a letter, and role-play an interview. These tasks would test their ability to use specific grammar and vocabulary (the dialogue completion), to use written English effectively (the letter-writing), and to understand and produce effective spoken English (the interview).

However, there is often a conflict between validity and reliability. The most reliable types of question are multiple-choice. The learners produce no English themselves, but only recognize correct language. Their answers can actually be marked by a computer, with no need for any subjective human judgements. The least reliable types of task include precisely the letter-writing and the interview role-play proposed above. These have to be marked subjectively by human beings.

The solution reached by many teachers and institutions is a compromise. Some exercises in the tests are of an objective, recognition type, for example, multiple-choice. These can cover a range of grammar and vocabulary as well as listening and reading comprehension. Other exercises and tasks are of a more subjective type, involving production and the communicative use of English. To reduce subjectivity, marking guides can be provided, which include the possible answers for fill-in and completion exercises, and criteria for marking compositions and interviews. This compromise also makes tests more practical. Multiple-choice exercises can usually be answered faster by learners and marked faster by teachers than production exercises and tasks.

Writing and evaluating achievement tests

As a teacher you may have to use course tests provided by your institution, or you may produce your own course tests. If the course tests are provided by the institution, you may still have opportunities to comment on them and make suggestions for modifications. In addition, you may want to produce a number of short progress tests. The following ideas should help you write, modify, or give opinions on tests.

Tests should normally be designed for specific teaching–learning situations. Some situations may call for more objective language exercises, others for more communicative tasks. Some situations may permit quite long tests, while others require short, easily administered tests because of a lack of time. Remember this when examining the sample tests presented below. They are simply examples, and neither may be a suitable model for your own teaching–learning situation.

Comparing tests

Test 1 and Test 2 below are both intended for the same teaching–learning situation—the end of a first-year secondary school course in Mexico. The course has communicative objectives in the four skills.

Task

Examine the two tests and decide which is more valid in general. Then examine each exercise or task and decide how reliable each one is likely to be.

Test 1

A **Complete these sentences with the correct forms for the Simple Present Tense:**

1 I _____ in the Miguel Hidalgo Secondary School. (study)
2 My English teacher _____ in a small yellow house. (live)
3 It _____ often _____ in the Sahara Desert. (rain)
4 Eskimos _____ often _____ ice-cream. (eat)
5 _____ you _____ music? Yes, I _____ . (like)
6 _____ the sun _____ a lot in the Arctic? No, it _____ . (shine)

B **Complete these sentences with the correct forms for the Present Progressive Tense:**

1 I _____ _____ an English test at the moment. (answer)
2 I _____ _____ _____ soccer. (play)
3 What _____ your father _____ at the moment? (do)
4 He _____ _____ . (work)
5 _____ the children _____ at the moment? (play)
6 No, they _____ . They _____ _____ . (study)

C **Complete this dialogue with:** *what time, how old, when, what, who,* **or** *where*:

John _____ are you?   Ann I'm twelve years old.
John _____ is your birthday.   Ann It's on August 12th.
John _____ do you live?   Ann I live in Holbrook Street.
John _____ instrument can you Ann I can play the piano.
    play?   _____ is it?
John It's eight o'clock.   Ann Eight o'clock! Oh! Goodbye!

D **Read the text and answer the questions.**

Mr Durán is teaching English at the moment. There are thirty students in his class. They can understand a lot of English, but they cannot speak much. Mr Durán teaches every day from Monday to Friday. He does not teach on Saturday, but he studies French. He can speak three languages. Let's all learn a second or third language!

---

1   What are Mr Durán's students doing now?

   _____

2   How many students are there in his class?

   _____

3   Can they speak a lot of English.

   _____

4   What does Mr Durán do on Fridays?

   _____

Test 2

A Listen to your teacher. Answer the questions.

[Teacher to say each question twice.]

1   I'm _____ years old _____   *How old are you?*
2   _____   *When is your birthday?*
3   _____   *What time do birthday parties usually start?*
4   _____   *Can you play the guitar?*
5   _____   *What do you eat and drink at parties?*
6   _____   *What are you doing at the moment?*

B Complete this conversation with expressions from the box.

Simon   (1) Hello, Mike. (2) _____ is it?
Mike   It's six (3) _____ . I have a karate class at six-thirty.
Simon   Yes, and I have a party at eight. It's Jenny's birthday party.
Mike   (4) _____ her birthday?
Simon   It's (5) _____ , but the party's today. (6) _____ to come?
Mike   Well, I don't have an invitation.
Simon   That's no problem. You (7) _____ , right?
Mike   Yes, and play the guitar. But I (8) _____ .
Simon   No problem. Take your guitar, sing and play, talk to people, eat and
        drink, and be happy! Just (9) _____ dance.
Mike   Well . . . I (10) _____ go to bed at nine-thirty on
        Thursdays . . .
Simon   Come on, Mike! (11) _____ go to your house and get your
        guitar.
Mike   Well . . . OK . . . and I can probably learn to dance!

June 25th   o'clock   When is   can't dance   What time   How old
don't   Let's   ~~Hello~~   are you doing   always   can sing   Do you want

---

C Complete the text of this radio commentary and interview:

Joe   Hello! Good afternoon! This (1) __is__ Joe Green on FM Radio
        42.9 in Ensenada, Baja California, Mexico. The sun usually (2)
        _____ here in June, but today (3) _____ raining. But
        Ensenada is beautiful, sun or rain. And it isn't cold today, it's (4)
        _____ . People are (5) _____ in the ocean and playing
        volleyball on the beach—in the rain! Here with me in Hotel Peñón
        are (6) _____ manager, Juan Gómez, and an American visitor,
        Janet Holt. Juan, (7) _____ it rain a lot in Ensenada?
Juan   Well, rain is very unusual in summer, but it often (8) _____ a lot
        in winter.
Joe   Janet, what are you (9) _____ in Ensenada? Are you on vacation?
Janet   No, (10) _____ studying marine mammals—dolphins, whales,
        seals. I (11) _____ at five o'clock every morning to observe the
        animals, while all the tourists are in bed!

D Complete the lists with more words or expressions:

Days: Monday, Tuesday, _____ , _____ , _____ , _____ , _____ .
Family: mother, _____ , _____ , _____ , _____ , _____ .
Activities: study, _____ , _____ , _____ , _____ , _____ .
Frequency: never, _____ , _____ , _____ , _____ , _____ .

E Read the article and answer the questions.

Chameleons are reptiles. They live in Africa, Asia, and parts of Europe. They
usually live in trees. There are different species of chameleon. Small species are
only 7 cms long, but big chameleons can be 60 cms! Chameleons usually eat
insects, but big species also eat birds and small animals. Chameleons are
famous for one special characteristic—they can change colour in response to
the conditions around them. They can be green among leaves, brown on a tree
trunk, yellow in the sun. This protects them, and it helps them trap insects.
They trap many victims! It is very difficult to see a chameleon, but they can
see very well. Their eyes function independently—they can look right and left
at the same time! They are very patient, and they trap insects with their long,
sticky tongue*.

* *lengua larga y pegajosa*

(i) Put a circle round T (true) or F (false):

1	Chameleons are mammals.	T	F
2	They live on three continents.	T	F
3	They are always green.	T	F
4	There are only two species.	T	F
5	They can look simultaneously in two directions.	T	F

(ii)   Answer with one, two, or three words:

    1 What are chameleons? _____

    2 What do they usually eat? _____

    3 What do big species eat? _____

    4 What colours can they be? _____

    5 What is their tongue like? _____

F Write five sentences of 4 to 8 words about yourself or your family.

1 My name is_____

2 _____

3 _____

4 _____

5 _____

Although Test 1 and Test 2 both test many of the same items (for example, the Simple Present, the Present Progressive, 'can', 'what time' 'how old', and weather vocabulary), there are many differences between them. Some of the most noticeable are:

a Test 2 is much longer than Test 1.

b Test 2 has listening comprehension and sentence writing, unlike Test 1, as well as more extended reading.

c Most of the exercises in Test 2 have a single topic or situation, while Exercises A and B in Test 1 consist mostly of unrelated sentences, and even the dialogue in Exercise C lacks normal conversational coherence.

d There seems to be more effort to make Test 2 interesting, especially the reading.

e Test 2 mixes grammatical structures naturally in discourse, while Test 1 has a separate exercise for each area of grammar.

f Test 2 does not state what is being tested, while Test 1 does, for example, 'Complete these sentences with the correct forms of the Simple Present Tense'.

g Most of the exercises in Test 2 have an example answer as well as clear instructions.

These differences all distinguish Test 2 as a much better final course test than Test 1. The inclusion of listening, writing, and more extended reading (b); the use of coherent topics and realistic situations (c); the effort to interest the learners in the content of the texts rather than always focusing their attention on the language (d); the natural mixing of different grammar areas (e), and the absence of grammatical terminology (f), all make Test 2 more valid for a course with communicative objectives. The extra length (a) and the clear instructions with examples (g) mean that Test 2 would probably also be more reliable.

Points (e) and (f) are quite significant. Exercises B and C in Test 2 produce evidence of whether the learners would be able to use grammar and vocabulary correctly in real conversations and other real communication situations. On the other hand, Exercises A, B, and C in Test 1 only produce evidence of whether the learners can produce correct forms when they are told what the grammar area is and are concentrating on that specific area only. Such exercises may be useful for early practice of a new grammar area, and perhaps in a progress test, but they are not really valid in the final test of a course with communicative objectives.

There is yet another reason for preferring Test 2. Tests can influence the way teachers teach and learners study. If teachers and learners know that the course tests will be like Test 1, they will tend to work one way, and if they know the course tests will be like Test 2, they will tend to work another way. Test 2 is likely to have a more positive influence—or *backwash* effect—on teaching and learning.

Test exercises and tasks

Test exercises or tasks can be classified in several ways. One way is by using scales like those in Figure 11.1.

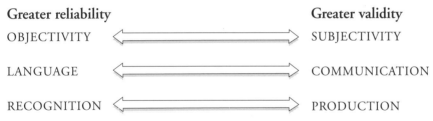

Greater reliability		Greater validity
OBJECTIVITY	⟵⟶	SUBJECTIVITY
LANGUAGE	⟵⟶	COMMUNICATION
RECOGNITION	⟵⟶	PRODUCTION

Figure 11.1: Scales for classifying test exercises or tasks

Test writers often combine exercises and tasks at both ends of these scales, with the aim of achieving a good balance of reliability and validity. The extremes on the left, especially objectivity, tend to give greater reliability. Examples from Tests 1 and 2 are 1, C and 2, B. The extremes on the right, especially communication, tend to give greater validity, though this depends partly on the type of course and the purpose of the test. The best examples from Tests 1 and 2 are both from Test 2—2, A and 2, F. The examples in Figure 11.2 go from the most objective to the most subjective. Many of these exercise and task types can be used either for testing language or for testing communication skills, but some are obviously more suitable for one purpose than the other.

OBJECTIVE

Select from different options
- true–false: for example, Test 2, E(i)
- words in a list or box: for example, Test 1, C
- multiple choice options: for example:

  I _____ in Veracruz.
  (a) lives (b) living (c) live

- matching: for example:

  1 I am _____   (a) speak French.
  2 I don't _____   (b) studying English.

Fill in spaces with one or more words
- assisted sentence fill-in: for example, Test 1, B
- open text fill-in: for example, Test 2, C.

Write answers to questions
- questions on a reading text: for example, Test 1, D
- spoken personal questions: for example, Test 2, A.

Write sentences or compositions
- separate sentences: for example, Test 2, F
- composition: for example: 'Write 80 to 100 words about a journey or holiday.'

Participate in an oral interview
- answer questions asked by the examiner, talk about a photograph, etc.

SUBJECTIVE

Figure 11.2: Test exercises and tasks classified on a scale of objectivity – subjectivity

Improving tests

It is extremely difficult to write good original tests. In fact, it is difficult and time-consuming even to write bad ones! For this reason it is usually better not to write new tests every time you need one. Instead, analyse the results of each test you use and decide which exercises and tasks, or parts of them, seem to work well and which do not. For example, if most of the learners do Exercises A, B, D, and E reasonably well, but they do Exercise C badly, change Exercise C but keep the rest. In this way you can develop better tests.

Evaluating learning, teaching, and courses

As we said in the first section of this chapter, evaluation in teaching English should be much more than giving tests to learners. Achieving improvement in teaching English is a matter of evaluating and developing syllabuses, materials, and teaching as well as testing. And real language learning is more than the ability to do test exercises and tasks. It is important to remind yourself again and again that not only learning needs to be evaluated. When satisfactory learning is obviously not taking place, teachers sometimes blame the learners, but it may not be their fault at all. There may be something wrong with the teaching, the testing, the course design or the way the courses are administered. Evaluation should really apply to the work of everyone in an educational institution, not just the learners.

Evaluating learning

Although they are useful, tests are only one way of evaluating learning. It is important to remember that you can also note how effectively the learners communicate in free conversation and groupwork, how well they use the language in homework compositions, and even ask them for their own impression of their progress. If it is possible where you teach, it is a good idea to combine 'teacher's impression' (i.e. your evaluation of each learner's overall performance during the course) with formal test results, for example, seventy per cent tests combined with thirty per cent teacher's impression.

Evaluating teaching

Learners' test results are one way to evaluate teaching. Good results should reflect good teaching, but the results are only as valid and reliable as the tests. Tests low in validity and/or reliability will give a false impression of teaching. In some institutions the learners take external proficiency tests at certain stages. These results are usually both reasonably valid and reliable. An institution or teacher with many learners getting increasingly good marks in the TOEFL tests, or passing successive levels of the UCLES exams can feel very satisfied.

But tests are not everything. Learners' opinions should also be taken into account. To some extent you can see their opinions on their faces and in their behaviour. But you can also give adults and even adolescents a simple, anonymous questionnaire, like the one below, to fill in at the end of each course:

Course assessment questionnaire

Course: _____

1 Did you enjoy the lessons?	yes so-so no
2 Did you learn a satisfactory amount of English?	yes so-so no
3 Did you have enough communicative practice of English?	yes so-so no

4 What did you particularly like about the course?

5 What didn't you like about the course?

In this way, the learners evaluate your teaching, just as you evaluate their learning. This is considered very healthy in many institutions and by many teachers. In some institutions it is standard practice, carried out at the end of every course.

You can also 'observe' yourself or ask a co-ordinator or colleague to observe you. The tendency in class observation is to focus critically on the teacher. But it is better to start by focusing on the learners. This will tell you more about the effect of your teaching than focusing on yourself. Obviously, you will also ask yourself why the learners responded the way they did, and that will lead you to useful reflection on the lesson plan, the techniques used, the relationship with the group, and so on. Observation is discussed further in Chapter 12.

Evaluating courses

Courses can be evaluated by using learners' test results, questionnaires given to learners and teachers, and class observation. Criteria for the evaluation of course syllabuses and course materials can also be useful (see Chapter 9), as well as criteria for the evaluation of tests (see page 174 above).

Summary

In Chapter 11 we have considered the following points:

Teaching, testing, and evaluation. Teaching should not be a continuous test for the learners, but you should be informally evaluating their performance and progress all the time. Testing is only one option in the evaluation of learning, which may also include the monitoring of learner performance in class, and learner self-evaluation. Teaching, teaching materials, and courses should be evaluated as well as learning.

Basic aspects of testing. There are five common types of test, each with a specific purpose: placement tests, diagnostic tests, progress tests, course tests, and proficiency tests. Achievement tests are valid when they contain only language and uses the learners have practised in the course, and employ only exercises and tasks that correspond to the general objectives and methodology of the course. Tests are reliable (i.e. the results can be trusted) when, for example, instructions are clear, exercises limit how learners can respond, and teachers follow the same marking criteria. The test should also be long enough to provide an adequate sample of learner performance. The reliability of a test also depends on how it is given, for example, time limits and good invigilation. High validity, especially for communicative courses, usually means low reliability, and vice versa. Good test writers try to balance validity and reliability.

Writing and evaluating achievement tests. In general, tests that conform to the criteria for validity and reliability are better than those that do not. They should generally test whether learners could use language in real life, not just whether they can do artificial exercises. Tests can influence positively or negatively the way teachers teach and learners study. This is called the backwash effect. There is a great variety of possible test exercises and tasks. They can be classified on scales of objectivity–subjectivity, recognition–production or language–communication, and different types of exercise are often combined to achieve a balance. Rather than always writing new tests, it is better to improve used tests by seeing from results which exercises and items work well and which do not and need changing.

Evaluating learning, teaching, and courses. Apart from testing, use class monitoring and learners' impressions to evaluate learning. Teaching can be evaluated through learners' course and external proficiency test results, questionnaires seeking learners' opinions, and class observation. Courses and teaching programmes can also be evaluated using all of the above, as well as criteria for the evaluation of syllabuses, materials, and tests. Evaluation should apply to the work of everyone in an educational institution, not just the learners.

Project

Developing course tests

Purpose: to develop the ability to produce, evaluate, and improve course tests.

Procedure:

1 Select a coursebook that you use now or might use in the future.
2 Study the contents up to a convenient point (for example, up to and including a review unit). If you are using the book now, choose a point that you will soon reach in the course.
3 Select four or five exercises that you consider cover the main points in the course up to that stage, and that are suitable for a test (for example, not repetitive structure drills).
4 Write the test, using parallel or similar exercises to those you have selected.
5 If you are able to give the test to a group of learners, do so and then analyse the results. Note which exercises and items in them the majority of the learners got right and which they got wrong. Consider how you would modify the test in its next version. If you are not able to give the test, leave it for a week without looking at it. Then go through it considering how it would seem to a real learner at that level and what changes might be appropriate.

12 DEVELOPMENT IN TEACHING ENGLISH

Introduction

In this chapter we look at how teachers have always tried to find more effective ways of working, usually adopting some kind of approach or method. We present a historical survey of widely used approaches and methods, looking at the principles underlying them and the typical activities and techniques used in each. Then we look at some interesting current movements in English teaching methodology. Finally, we consider ways in which you and your colleagues can develop individually and collectively as teachers.

Teachers and ways of teaching

Teachers have always tried to find more effective ways of carrying out their work. As a basis, most teachers adopt some kind of approach or method. In other words, they do not do things differently every class, in an erratic and unpredictable way. Instead, they use similar strategies class after class and respond in similar ways to recurring classroom situations.

Teachers may teach the way they do because they are imitating teachers they once had, or they have learnt from experience, or they are following a coursebook, or they are applying the recommendations of a training course. In the first two cases, their approach or method may be quite idiosyncratic, especially if they teach in an isolated situation. In the last two cases, they will probably be following an approach or method similar to one used by many other teachers.

Approach and method

Approaches and methods are both usually based on fairly definite views about:

- the nature of language
- the nature of language learning
- the nature of teaching.

An *approach* is based mainly on theories of the nature of language and the nature of language learning. These theories, implicit or explicit, establish a kind of 'philosophy of language teaching'. Here are outlines of two hypothetical approaches:

Approach X

A language is a system of rules for the construction of correct sentences. These rules are specified in good grammar books, and, for many languages—but unfortunately not English—by an Academy. Languages are learnt properly by memorizing the rules and applying them when constructing sentences in writing or speech. One of the best ways of learning a foreign language is to translate backwards and forwards between that language and one's L1, taking care not to confuse the rules of the two languages. Intelligent, diligent people learn foreign languages faster and better than others.

Approach Y

A language is a system of communication, in which linguistic forms and structures convey messages and intentions in specific contexts or situations. There are variations in languages, for example, formal and informal styles, and regional and social dialects. Languages are acquired by hearing them used in communication and using them yourself. Formal study of a foreign language (for example, memorizing rules and drilling) is largely a waste of time. You have to use the language in real communication, and go through a slow, subconscious process, making many errors. Anyone can acquire a foreign language if they are in the right environment and are motivated.

The different implications for teaching of each of these two approaches are clear. An approach provides orientation for teachers, but it may not give many detailed specifications of what and how to teach. That is the realm of methods.

A *method* has a general approach behind it—a theory of language and of language learning—but it goes into more detail about such things as the syllabus, learning activities, and teaching techniques. Different methods may have essentially the same approach behind them. Some methods—or the inventors of some methods—are quite dogmatic about what teachers should and should not do. Many teaching institutions prefer to establish a general approach but not specify a particular method, leaving a lot of freedom of action in the classroom, including the freedom to experiment. Others prefer to regulate what happens in the classroom very strictly, with a well-defined method and intensive teacher training in that specific method.

A survey of approaches and methods

Approaches and methods in teaching English can be seen as a historical sequence of revolutions and evolutions, and also as a growing range of teaching options. New ideas and information from linguistics, psychology, and pedagogy have certainly meant that foreign language teaching has evolved since the middle of the nineteenth century. If we are not teaching better now than in 1850, we should be. However, new approaches and methods have never totally invalidated or replaced previous ones—despite the attitude of some inventors of new methods that Old Method X was totally wrong and their New Method Y is totally effective.

Whatever the inventors of new methods say, many teachers continue to use activities and techniques that have passed out of fashion. Sometimes this is the result of ignorance rather than informed professional judgement. But other teachers, who are trained and well-informed, also take ideas from unfashionable methods because they seem appropriate for their own teaching–learning situation. This is known as eclecticism. Eclectic approaches, based on well-informed views of the nature of language, language learning, and language teaching, and a good analysis of the specific teaching–learning situation, are considered by many English teaching professionals to be the best.

The historical sequence of the main approaches and methods, and therefore some of the main methodological options available today, is presented in Figure 12.1.

In the outlines of the approaches and methods which follow, the main aspects focused on are their:

– view of language
– view of language learning
– view of the roles of the teacher
– view of the roles of the learners
– typical teaching–learning activities.

1850 1860 1870 1880 1890 1900 1910 1920 1930 1940 1950 1960 1970 1980 1990

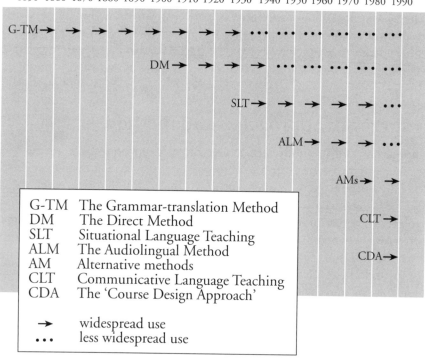

G-TM	The Grammar-translation Method
DM	The Direct Method
SLT	Situational Language Teaching
ALM	The Audiolingual Method
AM	Alternative methods
CLT	Communicative Language Teaching
CDA	The 'Course Design Approach'
→	widespread use
...	less widespread use

Figure 12.1: Historical sequence of the main approaches and methods

The Grammar-translation Method

This method arose out of the traditional teaching of classical Latin and Greek, when living languages began to be widely taught in the nineteenth century. It was the dominant method until the end of the century and has continued to be used in one form or another until the present day. But it has long been 'out of fashion'. It has many similarities with Approach X, outlined above.

Languages are seen as systems of rules for the construction of correct sentences. Writing is considered to be the superior form of a language. Languages are believed to be learnt best by memorizing the rules, along with bilingual vocabulary lists, and applying them when constructing sentences, mostly in writing. Translation is considered one of the best ways of practising the application of rules, as well as the transformation of sentences from, for example, Present Tense to Past Tense, or Active to Passive. The teacher's role is to explain grammar rules and the meaning of words in the learners' native language, organize practice (for example, the recitation of rules and translation), and correct learners' mistakes. The learners' role is to pay careful attention to the teacher's explanations and corrections, memorize rules and vocabulary lists, and carefully do the practice tasks the teacher sets.

The Direct Method

This method developed as a revolution against the Grammar-translation Method at the end of the nineteenth century. It was based to some extent on the new sciences of the nineteenth century, especially linguistics and psychology. It has many similarities with Approach Y, outlined above.

Languages are seen as systems of communication, primarily oral, in which words are used together in sentences, and sentences are used together in discourse. Languages are believed to be learnt best in a natural way, by hearing words and sentences in context and imitating what you hear. The learner's L1 should be avoided at all costs, and meaning should be conveyed through showing, drawing, miming or demonstrating things. Asking and answering questions is considered one of the best forms of practice, with the learners speaking as much as possible. The teacher needs to be active, demonstrating the language, organizing practice, and correcting the learners. The learners' role is to listen carefully, imitate, and participate as much as possible in the oral practice of the language.

In spite of the contrast between the Direct Method and the Grammar-translation Method, some teachers began to combine elements of both in their teaching, for example, Grammar-translation Method presentation followed by Direct Method practice, or Direct Method presentation and practice followed by a Grammar-translation Method grammar summary. Also, these teachers would progressively eliminate the use of the L1 from the classroom at higher levels. This combination of methods could be seen as an early form of the eclecticism that continues to this day.

Situational Language Teaching

This method was developed in the 1920s and 1930s by British applied linguists who were not entirely happy with the Direct Method. It continued developing up to the 1970s. It shares many views about language and learning with the Direct Method, and is equally opposed to the Grammar-translation Method. In its origins, it was partly a response to the weaker aspects of the Direct Method, and partly a development which arose from theoretical concepts in British linguistics, especially the idea that language can be properly understood only in the context of real situations of use.

Situational Language Teaching takes the Direct Method idea of presentation and practice using objects, pictures, and demonstration a step further, doing presentation and practice within a single coherent 'situation' whenever possible. Ideally, situations should be realistic, like shopping or learning to drive. The learners' sentences are judged on 'truth' in relation to the situation as well as on linguistic correctness. This kind of practice is considered better preparation for the real use of the language than the production of situationally unrelated examples of a structure. It is also believed that interesting or humorous situations motivate the learners.

The Direct Method was weak in syllabus design and classroom techniques. Situational Language Teaching approaches the selection and grading of the language content of courses very clearly. The grammar content is organized in terms of sentence patterns, beginning with the ones thought to be the easiest, commonest, and most useful. These sentence patterns are the basis of substitution tables, and one of the most basic activities in Situational Language Teaching is *substitution practice* in which many sentences of the same pattern are produced by the learners, including questions and answers. As in the Direct Method, oral practice is the first stage for each new language item and is generally emphasized, but Situational Language Teaching sees a more important supporting role for reading and writing than the Direct Method does.

The Audiolingual Method

This method grew indirectly out of a programme developed by American linguists and psychologists for the US Army during the Second World War. But it really took shape when American Structural Linguistics and Behaviourist Psychology were adopted as the twin foundations of a 'scientific' approach to foreign language teaching in the late 1950s. It is similar in many ways to Situational Language Teaching, but there are some notable differences.

Two of the main activities of the Audiolingual Method are dialogue repetition and memorization, and substitution drilling. The dialogues are often little more than vehicles for pronunciation practice with a few contextualized models of the new structure. The substitution drilling is often uncontextualized manipulation of structures, and is very intensive and extensive. In the Audiolingual Method, correct production by learners should always be praised (reinforced) and incorrect production instantly and firmly corrected.

Alternative methods

'Alternative methods' here refers to several methods and one approach developed between the mid-1960s and the early 1980s that have been quite influential, although they have never been widely used. In some ways they can be seen as products of the search for the 'perfect method'. We will focus here only on a few key features of each.

Total Physical Response (TPR)

TPR was developed by James Asher in the USA from the mid-1960s. It is suitable for beginners' courses only, and later needs to be supplemented by activities and techniques from other methods. It aims to develop listening comprehension before production, to associate language with action, and to reduce stress in language learning. In these ways, it tries to replicate typical features of L1 acquisition. Most other methods demand instant speaking from the learners rather than providing them with extensive listening practice first. Most other methods also connect language with language (for example, model and repetition, question and answer) rather than with action, and often create a lot of tension in the learners. TPR connects language with action by getting the learners to do what the teacher tells them to.

The Silent Way

The Silent Way was developed by Caleb Gattegno in the USA from the early 1970s. It contrasts almost totally with TPR. Instead of giving extensive active listening comprehension practice, the teacher is silent for most of the time, giving only single examples of new sentence structures and then getting different learners to attempt to reproduce the sentence and produce similar ones. The method is based on the hypothesis that discovery and problem-solving produce much better learning than imitation and repetition. Learners must concentrate and usually struggle a bit to benefit from the method. Teachers need special training in the use of Silent Way materials and techniques.

Suggestopedia

Suggestopedia was developed by Georgi Lozanov in Bulgaria from the early 1970s, and then by Jane Bancroft in Canada and others elsewhere. Its main concern is the facilitation of memorization. In foreign language teaching, Suggestopedia is applied largely to the memorization of 'interesting' texts in the L2. Learners are provided with an L1 translation of the texts so that they have a fair understanding of what they are memorizing. These memorized texts are then used as the basis for other language analysis and practice activities. Memory is facilitated by relaxing surroundings (for example, pleasant decor and comfortable furniture), soothing background music, and confident, authoritative reading and behaviour by the teacher. The teacher's reading of the text to be memorized should be matched to the rhythm of the background music.

Community Language Learning

This method was developed by Charles Curran in the USA from the mid-1970s. The teacher is at the learners' service, to help them achieve their own goals. Learning is seen as personal development, not the achievement of objectives imposed from outside by the teacher or the institution. The learners sit in a circle, with the teacher standing outside it. Any learner can volunteer to ask a question or make a statement (in the L1 at beginner level). The teacher repeats this question or statement in the L2 as many times as the learner wishes to hear it. Then the learner says it, recording it onto a cassette. Another learner responds to the question or statement (again in the L1 at beginner level), listens to the teacher repeating the response in the L2, and records it onto the cassette. In this way, a conversation in the L2 among the learners is slowly built up on the cassette. The teacher then replays the whole recording and the learners listen to their 'conversation'. The teacher selects some sentences from the conversation and writes them on the board for analysis and discussion of the language. A notable feature of this method is that the learners, not the teacher or the institution, create the syllabus according to their own interests and concerns.

The Natural Approach

The Natural Approach was developed by Tracy Terrell in the USA from the late 1970s, later in collaboration with Stephen Krashen. Like the Direct Method, the Natural Approach is organized on the general lines of Approach Y above. Languages are seen mainly as a means of communication in specific situations. They are acquired by hearing them used in communication and using them yourself. Formal study of a foreign language is largely a waste of time. You have to use the language in real communication, and go through a slow, subconscious process, making many errors. The Natural Approach works at promoting subconscious *acquisition*, and relegates conscious *learning* to a minor role. It begins with TPR activities, providing the learners with a lot of comprehensible listening input related to actions. In later stages, it continues to use activities associated with other approaches and methods, especially the Direct Method, Situational Language Teaching, and Communicative Language Teaching. In this respect it is eclectic. The Natural

Approach does not work systematically through a predetermined language syllabus, but progresses by focusing on communication in areas of need and interest to the learners. It emphasizes the importance of reducing stress and anxiety, and promoting the learners' motivation and self-confidence.

One reason why these alternative methods are not widely used is that they all require highly-trained teachers with ample time for lesson preparation. Most also require other special conditions, for example, small groups of mature, motivated learners and specific types of classroom. Another reason is that most of them depend on a single, strong theory of learning, and are therefore out of tune with current eclecticism. However, they do suggest considerations, activities, and techniques that can often be usefully incorporated into eclectic teaching, for example:

– More, active listening practice and less teacher-controlled oral repetition.
– More involvement of the learners in discovery and problem-solving activities, and less passive listening to the teacher's explanations and corrections.
– More consideration of the learners' physical and emotional states.
– More consideration of the learners' real needs and wants, and less obsession with 'getting through' the syllabus.
– More effort to reduce anxiety and increase self-confidence in the learners.
– More attention to the communicative use of language, and less obsession with constant formal accuracy.

Communicative Language Teaching

This approach grew out of new theories of language and language learning that developed in the 1960s and 1970s in Britain, the USA, and elsewhere, as well as new classroom procedures. It is probably the approach most used by trained language teachers today. But it is implemented in very different ways by different teachers working in different contexts. It is an approach with wide variations, not a well-defined method. By its very nature it is eclectic.

In principle, even if not always in practice, language is seen in terms of:

– What we do with utterances, their specific communicative functions (for example, informing, enquiring, ordering, and inviting) and not just in terms of the formal structure of sentences and their basic meanings (see Chapter 2).

- How we really use language in authentic discourse—for example, when we say:

> A Hey, you're wanted in Room 13.
> B Where is it?
> A On the next floor.
> B Thanks.

and when we say:

> A Excuse me. Could you tell me where Room 13 is?
> B Yes, it's on the next floor.
> A Thank you.
> B Not at all.

as well as the fact that we seldom, if ever, say:

> A Where is Room 13?
> B Room 13 is on the next floor.

(See Chapters 3 and 5.)

Also in principle, even if not always in practice, language learning is seen as essentially a long process of acquisition through exposure to and communicative use of the language, with many inevitable mistakes. However, conscious effort and a wide range of formal learning activities can significantly speed up and improve the learners' progress, especially in the case of adolescents and adults. Repetition practice is used in most Communicative Language Teaching, but it is normally of the Situational Language Teaching type—situationally contextualized and meaningful. Interesting, motivating communicative skills work, including integrated skills work, is emphasized as one of the best ways to promote both subconscious acquisition and conscious learning of the language. Communicative activities inevitably mean that the teacher relaxes control over what the learners hear, say, read, write—and think—and so the learners have to take some control over their own learning. In Communicative Language Teaching, this independence from the teacher, or learner *autonomy*, is generally considered essential for success in language learning.

The 'Course Design Approach'

The 'Course Design Approach' is a term we have invented for this book. The principle is that teachers should find out exactly who they are teaching in every course they give; for example, what the learners' interests are, their learning styles, and their current or possible future uses of English. They should then plan and run lessons always taking this knowledge into account. It refers in part to the English for Specific Purposes (ESP) movement that began in the late 1960s. ESP recognizes the different needs of different groups of learners, and focuses on the design of appropriate courses for them. What kind of course is appropriate for a group of medical researchers with a knowledge of no more than basic English grammar and vocabulary? What kind of course is appropriate for a group of tourist resort waiters with virtually no English at all? Obviously, the two groups need very different courses, especially if they both have an immediate need for English in their work and limited time for study. These are extreme examples, but every teaching–learning situation calls for at least some adaptation of teaching methodology and coursebook materials.

What works best?

To conclude this survey of approaches and methods, a general point should be made. The Grammar-translation Method, the Direct Method, Situational Language Teaching, the Audiolingual Method, TPR, the Silent Way, Community Language Learning, Suggestopedia, the Natural Approach, and Communicative Language Teaching have all contributed potentially useful ideas to English teaching. But developments in linguistics, psychology, pedagogy, and second language acquisition research have cast light on what is more likely and less likely to work. At a minimum, we have learnt that an approach on the general lines of Communicative Language Teaching is much more likely to work in the majority of teaching–learning situations than the Grammar-translation Method or the Audiolingual Method.

Current developments

Although we may not see any distinctive new approach or method for a long time, new ideas are continually arising. Some are relevant to virtually all English teaching, but others may apply only to specific teaching–learning situations. Yet others may soon be forgotten. A few ideas that may have a lasting impact are presented in the following sections. Some of these have already been mentioned in this book.

Learner-centred Teaching

Most approaches and methods have assumed for convenience that all learners are more or less the same. But teachers know this is not true. Research is showing how different successful language learners can be, although the most successful learners do tend to have certain things in common, for example, they are motivated, they combine analytical and communicative strategies, and they exploit opportunities to practise. The new awareness among teachers of learner differences has led to a number of important developments in English teaching.

Many teachers now try to find out about individual learners' motivations, needs, interests, and learning styles. *Learning styles* are, for example, a preference for listening–speaking activities rather than reading–writing activities, for language-focused rather than communication-focused activities, or for *lockstep* and groupwork rather than individual work. These teachers then prepare lesson plans that take into account the commonest motivations, needs, and interests of the learners, and also offer different learners in the group opportunities to work in the ways they find most comfortable and useful. This involves substituting, supplementing, or adapting coursebook material, including different types of activity and interaction in lessons, and working with learners on an individual basis whenever possible.

However, some learners seem to be unsuccessful because their learning styles and strategies are simply not very effective. Many teachers now spend time on *learner training*, helping learners to be more aware of themselves as learners, and how they can develop whatever strengths they have and overcome their weaknesses. Overcoming weaknesses usually means adopting strategies used by successful learners, such as not being obsessed with total accuracy on the one hand or being satisfied with primitive 'me-Tarzan-you-Jane' communication on the other. Many learner training activities can be incorporated into normal lesson plans, especially at upper elementary and intermediate levels; for example, the use of questionnaires and discussions about aspects of language learning.

A characteristic of highly successful learners is that they are autonomous. They do not depend much on teachers. They themselves decide how to study outside class and even how to work in class. They do not constantly depend on teacher feedback and approval. Teachers who organize a lot of free work in class, whether lockstep, in groups or individual, promote learner autonomy. Also, many institutions now provide self-access facilities such as a library, computers, and audio- and video-cassette players which learners can use.

Task-based Learning

The idea of getting learners to acquire English in the process of doing other tasks was developed in India by N. S. Prabhu in the 1980s. His 'Procedural Syllabus' consists, not of language items, but of tasks requiring increasingly complex use of language. The problem-solving or practical tasks, usually done in groups, were designed to interest and challenge the learners sufficiently to get them to use the English they already knew and incorporate new items provided by input materials and the teacher. That led to a general proposal for Task-based Learning, suitable, in principle, for use in most English teaching situations. A three-stage procedure is commonly recommended:

1 Pre-task
– Introduction to the topic and task
– Provision of useful input (listening, reading, brainstorming, etc.)
– If necessary, reactivation or provision of essential language
– Definition of the task (objectives, procedures, time limits, etc.)

2 Task
– Planning the task
– Doing the task
– Reporting on the task or presenting the product of the task
  [teacher monitoring and guiding as necessary all the time]

3 Post-task
– Focus on the language used
– Practice of the language as necessary
– Retrospective discussion of the task—awareness-raising

It is important to emphasize that tasks in Task-based Learning should have very clear objectives and conclude with a very tangible sense of achievement for the learners.

It is not generally suggested by those who have developed Task-based Learning that courses should consist entirely of tasks. That could become tedious for both learners and teachers. Task-based learning can be used with other approaches in a number of ways, for example, as an alternative way of introducing new language, to do language review and remedial work, and to do skills and general language development work.

Developing as a teacher

It is very important to get initial training and, if possible, a recognized teaching qualification. However, initial training should be the beginning, not the end, of your professional development. Teacher development programmes can facilitate regular contact with new ideas and their classroom application. Development options can be grouped into three broad categories: Self-development, Co-operative Development, and Formal Development.

Self-development

Constant reflection

Probably the most important and profitable way to develop as a teacher is to think about what you have done in each lesson you teach. You could ask yourself the following questions:

- How effective was the lesson in general?
- How did the learners respond to the different activities?
- What good bits were there, and why were they good? How could I develop them further?
- What weak bits were there, and why were they weak? How could I have handled them better?

You can note down a few observations at the bottom of your plan immediately after the lesson. You can then use these notes to reflect upon individual lessons, and also to see what patterns—positive and negative—there are in your teaching. Experience is really useful only if you constantly reflect upon it. This may be difficult at first, with little to compare your limited experience with. But as you acquire experience in reflecting upon teaching as well as actually teaching, it becomes easier to understand the underlying reasons for your successes and your failures.

Diary writing

Reflection can be based on more than a few notes and vague memories. Keeping a diary of your teaching activities over a whole term can really help you to appreciate how much your learners and you yourself have progressed, and why. If you find that the story you are telling in your diary is not very positive, this can motivate you to make changes and explore new options. In this way, you can begin to know yourself professionally—what you are good at and what you need to work on more.

Recording lessons

Sometimes it is difficult to remember what actually happened in a lesson, even immediately after it has ended. One way to overcome this problem is to record lessons or parts of lessons. Simply switch on a cassette recorder at the point of the lesson you have chosen, perhaps the very beginning, and try to forget it is recording. You can then replay the recording at home, and analyse and reflect on what you hear.

As a result of this analysis and reflection, you may find that you want to try and do some of the following things:

- Reduce the amount of talking you do and elicit more from the learners, listening more patiently to them.
- Make the talking you do sound more suitable and interesting for your learners according to their age and other characteristics.
- Make your instructions and explanations clearer and more effective.
- Eliminate mistakes in English that you have been making repeatedly without realizing it, even though you recognize them when you hear them.
- Make your interaction with the learners more natural.

After you have worked on your plans for change for a while, you can record some lessons again and check on your progress.

Reading

One of the best ways of keeping up with developments in the profession is to read English teaching books, journals, newsletters, and Internet publications. If the institution where you work does not already have such resources, you may be able to persuade the management to make some of them available. A small teacher's library does not have to cost much. The core can be a selection of basic English teaching textbooks like this one, and others on specific areas such as the teaching of vocabulary, grammar, listening, speaking, reading, and writing. A selection of modern coursebooks containing recent teaching ideas can also be very useful. You may also occasionally be able to invest in books for yourself, or subscribe to journals such as *ELT Journal* or *English Teaching Forum*. A number of useful books are listed in 'Sources and further reading' at the end of this book.

Co-operative development

Sharing with colleagues

The teachers in an institution ought to communicate with one another, principally for the sake of the learners. It is a matter of professional ethics that the staff of any educational institution should work together, not against one another or in isolation. The benefits of this can be enormous for teachers as well as learners. Sharing experiences and ideas with colleagues increases your own experience and ideas, and it can give you a better perspective on your own work. You can measure your achievement against a more objective standard.

Place:	Date:	Time:
Level:		Number of learners:

Were the learners:

paying attention?	always	usually	sometimes	never
participating?	always	usually	sometimes	never
showing enthusiasm?	always	usually	sometimes	never
confused?	never	seldom	sometimes	often
practising English?	continually	a lot	occasionally	very little
communicating in English?	continually	a lot	occasionally	very little

Was the lesson:

well planned and structured?	very	moderately	not very	not at all
varied in activities?	very	moderately	not very	not at all
varied in interactions?	very	moderately	not very	not at all
balanced in accuracy/fluency?	very	moderately	not very	not at all
appropriate for the group?	very	moderately	not very	not at all
enjoyable to watch?	very	moderately	not very	not at all

Was the teacher:

organized and confident?	totally	very	moderately	not very	
communicating in English?	always	usually	sometimes	seldom	never
showing enthusiasm?	always	usually	sometimes	seldom	never
dominating the class?	never	occasionally	frequently	continually	
clear and effective?	always	usually	sometimes	seldom	never
encouraging the students?	always	usually	sometimes	seldom	never

Other observations and comments:

Peer observation

In many places it is almost a tradition to teach behind closed doors. Some 'very experienced' teachers have never in their professional lives seen another teacher at work, nor had feedback from anyone observing their teaching. This lack of shared experience greatly restricts professional development: even occasional observation of another teacher's lessons can greatly promote it. Perhaps you are sometimes observed by a co-ordinator. This can be very useful if the co-ordinator is professional and sensitive rather than just authoritarian. Unfortunately, authoritarian 'inspection' of classes makes many teachers see any observer as a threat. But peer observation between colleagues can be friendly and collaborative, and therefore often more acceptable and useful. Visiting a colleague's classroom, and just sitting and observing, allows you to notice many things that you are simply not aware of while you are busy teaching.

When observing, it is usually best to focus on only one or two aspects of the lesson. And remember that it is often better to watch the learners rather than the teacher. What the learners do and do not do is probably the best indication of how effective the teaching is. Your comments to your colleague after the lesson will almost certainly be useful if you focus on the learners, since teachers often fail to notice many aspects of learner behaviour because they are too busy running the lesson. In addition, make sure you comment on the best aspects of the lesson. Most of us need as much realistic encouragement as we can get. Opposite is an example of the kind of form you can use when observing a lesson. The first section focuses on the learners only. You can use that section alone, one of the other sections alone, or all three sections together.

Formal development

In-service training programmes

In almost every professional or technical field nowadays, the initial training and knowledge you acquire will not be sufficient for you to function satisfactorily for the whole of your working career. If you also have an ambition to rise in the profession, in-service training is essential. Many professionals nowadays are already thinking of their next course before they graduate from their initial training programme. A dynamic career development programme may well look something like Figure 12.2. Remember that the in-service training you undertake, apart from improving your teaching skills, will also raise your professional status and increase your value in the job market. It is a serious option for most teachers, and more and more employers are now demanding it. It is also worth mentioning that the best in-service training courses are often quite difficult to enter. The better your English is and the more you have pursued self-development and co-operative development, the better your chances of acceptance will be.

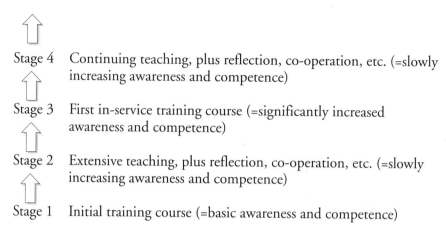

Stage 4   Continuing teaching, plus reflection, co-operation, etc. (=slowly increasing awareness and competence)

Stage 3   First in-service training course (=significantly increased awareness and competence)

Stage 2   Extensive teaching, plus reflection, co-operation, etc. (=slowly increasing awareness and competence)

Stage 1   Initial training course (=basic awareness and competence)

Figure 12.2: A career development programme

Conferences, seminars, and short courses

Apart from full development programmes, there are many conferences, seminars, and short courses for teachers of English. These events give you the opportunity to hear first-hand what is happening in English language teaching worldwide, often with presentations by leading professionals. They also allow you to exchange experiences and ideas with other teachers working in a similar situation to your own. And they remind any isolated teachers who attend these events that they are not alone. They belong to a large and developing profession.

Summary

In Chapter 12 we have considered the following points:

Teachers and ways of teaching. In trying to find effective ways of working, most teachers adopt some kind of approach or method. They teach quite consistently, following certain principles and using certain strategies. If what they do is based on recommendations in a coursebook or training course, they are probably using a fairly standard approach or method. An approach establishes principles related to the nature of language, learning, and teaching, but does not usually specify activities and techniques. A method establishes principles, but it also specifies or recommends certain activities and techniques. Some teachers and institutions follow a specific method strictly, but many others prefer the freedom and flexibility of an eclectic approach suited to their specific teaching situation.

A survey of approaches and methods. From the middle of the nineteenth century to the present day, approaches and methods have tended to move from an idealized formal view of language to a realistic communicative view, and from an academic view of language learning to an experiential view (acquisition through use of the language). The focus of classroom activity has also tended to move from teacher explanation, teacher supervision of exercises, and teacher correction of errors to more learner involvement and learner autonomy.

Current developments. Recognition of the differences among learners has encouraged teachers to take learners' motivations, needs, interests, and learning styles into account, and also try to individualize learning. 'Poor learners' may become more successful with learner training, including encouragement to be more autonomous. Task-based Learning opposes the pattern in which new language items are explicitly presented and practised. In Task-based Learning the emphasis is not on language items, but on doing attractive or useful tasks that require the use of those items. It can be used in Communicative Language Teaching as an alternative way of working on new language, and for consolidation or remedial work on language. Teachers need to keep up with new ideas like these and be prepared to change their way of teaching.

Developing as a teacher. Initial training should be the beginning, not the end, of your professional development. Self-development can be promoted by reflecting on your teaching, developing what consistently seems to go well, and experimenting with alternative approaches to what consistently seems to go badly. Diaries and recordings of your own lessons can help you notice things you would not notice otherwise. Co-operative development can be promoted by sharing ideas and experiences with colleagues. Peer observation is a good way of sharing experience, and is usually more supportive than supervisory observation. Formal development is now virtually essential during almost every stage of a teacher's career. Apart from actual in-service courses, there are many conventions, seminars, and short courses for teachers of English. Finally, professional reading is one of the best ways to extend your knowledge and keep up with new ideas.

Project A

Developing an awareness of appropriate methodology

Purpose: to develop the ability to adapt to different teaching–learning situations using eclectic methodology.

Procedure:

1 Examine two or three coursebooks designed for distinct teaching–learning situations, for example, a primary beginners' course, an adults' elementary course, and an ESP course (English for doctors, engineers, etc.).
2 Note the most striking differences in the materials and activities, and try to relate these to:
    a   the approaches and methods described in this chapter.
    b   the teaching–learning situation the coursebooks are intended for.
3 Select one unit from a book you were not previously familiar with. Consider how exactly you would use it in class—what you would omit, substitute, supplement, or adapt. Consider also what kind of relationship you should try to establish with the learners.

Project B

Developing as a reflective teacher

Purpose: to develop a reflective approach to teaching.

Procedure:

1 Select two or three questions from the list below, or write your own questions:
    a How do beginners react to the instant, exclusive use of the foreign language when you keep it simple and try to help them understand?
    b What kind of lesson plans and activities are most appropriate in the first classes with beginners?
    c How do learners accustomed mainly to grammar explanation or drilling react to extended communication skills sessions?
    d How do specific topics and/or situations (from the syllabus, the book, or specially selected for the learners by you) affect learners' attitudes and participation?
2 Plan how you could find some kind of answer to your selected questions in the course of your teaching during the next few months. Implement the plan. Note and then reflect on the results. What implications are there for your teaching in the future?

GLOSSARY

accuracy: Grammatical and lexical correctness. Accuracy practice is intended to promote this. Compare *fluency*.

achievement: Reaching the objectives of a lesson, unit, or course. An *achievement test* is intended to evaluate this.

acquiring/acquisition: Picking up a language subconsciously by using it to communicate, e.g. immigrants mostly acquire their new language through daily use. Contrast *learning*.

active vocabulary: Words learners are able to use in their speech and writing. Contrast *passive vocabulary*.

activity: Something learners do in order to promote learning or *acquisition*, e.g. a speaking activity or a reading comprehension activity.

aid: Support for teaching, e.g. pictures, cassette player, video.

antonym: Word opposite in meaning to another word, e.g. 'big' is an antonym of 'small'.

approach: Way of teaching based on ideas about language, learning, and teaching. See also method.

autonomy: See *independence*.

backwash effect: How tests influence teaching and studying, e.g. grammar tests can have a negative backwash effect on teachers and learners in communicative courses.

cognate: Word with a similar form and meaning in two different languages, e.g. 'doctor' is a *cognate* in most languages.

communication/communicative: Related to purposeful transfer of information or ideas, e.g. in the classroom, questions and answers like 'How many windows are there?' 'There are two', is not communicative; but talking about restaurants in the learners' city may be.

connotation: Secondary meaning, often either positive or negative, e.g. 'skinny' means thin, but it has a negative connotation–'thin and unattractive'.

construct validity: A test has construct validity when it contains only tasks like those used in teaching the course.

content validity: A test has content validity when it tests only what has been taught.

context: What surrounds something, e.g. 'It is hard' may mean 'It is difficult' or 'It is rigid' according to the context of the sentence. We also talk of a *teaching context*.

cue: Something teachers do or use to elicit language from learners, e.g. asking questions and showing pictures can both be effective cues in a *drill*.

discourse: Language in communicative use. Conversation is the commonest form of discourse.

drill/drilling: Repetitive teacher-controlled form of practice. See also *substitution practice* and *pattern*.

elicit/elicitation: Getting ideas and/or language from somebody, e.g. teachers often start courses by eliciting personal information from the learners such as 'I'm _____ years old'.

ELT: English Language Teaching.

error: Incorrect form or use of language that a learner cannot correct because he or she does not know the correct form or use. Compare *mistake* and *slip*.

evaluation: Measuring of strengths and weaknesses. You can evaluate courses and teachers as well as learning and learners. See also *test/testing*.

flashcard: Card with a picture or word on it used as a *cue*.

feedback: Informative responses to what learners say or do, e.g. a nod, smile, puzzled frown, or clarifying question are all useful feedback to learners.

fill-in: Exercise with spaces for learners to put in a word or phrase.

fluency: Ability to communicate with little hesitation. Fluency practice is intended to promote the use of language for real communication. Compare *accuracy*.

fossilization: Fixing of certain mistakes and errors in a learner's English, especially intermediate and advanced learners.

function: Specific communicative use of language, e.g. accusing, denying, confessing, explaining, and apologizing are related communicative functions.

functional-grammatical item: Language structure with a typical *function*, e.g. 'I'd [+ verb], if I were you' for giving advice.

gist: General idea of a text. A teacher might ask a class to read a text quickly 'for gist' before studying it more closely.

goal: Long-term results aimed at, e.g. what you want the learners to know and be able to do at the end of a course or series of courses. Compare *objective.*

groupwork: Activity, usually communicative, done by groups of three or more.

highlight: Emphasize key grammatical elements, e.g. 'He's sleeping: He *is sleeping.*'

independence: Ability to learn and use language without the help of a teacher; also referred to as *autonomy.*

information gap: Situation, normal in *communication*, when one person knows something another does not. It can form a good basis for communicative activities.

input: Language heard or read by learners.

integrated skills: Lesson, or section of a lesson, in which several skills are naturally combined.

interaction: Pattern of communication and relationship between people. Teacher controlled *drilling* and communicative *pairwork* are contrasting types of interaction.

L1: First language, native language.

L2: Second language; sometimes defined specifically as a language learnt in a country where it is spoken.

learner training: Helping learners become aware of their *learning style* and how they can make it more effective.

learning: Conscious process, usually involving formal study. Contrast *acquisition.*

learning style: A preference for learning in certain ways, e.g. through listening and conversation, or through formal explanation and written exercises.

lockstep: The whole class attending to the same activity, e.g. teacher presentation, drilling. Compare *groupwork, pairwork.*

method: Way of teaching based on ideas about language, learning, and teaching, with specific indications about *activities* and *techniques* to be used. See also *approach.*

mistake: Incorrect form or use of language that a learner can correct because he or she knows the correct form or use. Compare *error* and *slip.*

model: Example of a language pattern used in *presentation* or clarification, e.g. a model of the 'going to' future for the learners to imitate.

monitor: Observe and supervise an activity, e.g. a teacher might monitor *pairwork.*

multiple choice: Type of exercise in which the learners have to choose the best of several answers, e.g. They _____ Australian. (a) am (b) is (c) are.

nomination: Selection of learner to say or do something, e.g. you can nominate a learner to answer a question by saying his or her name, or smiling at him or her.

objective: Short or medium-term results aimed at, e.g. what you want the learners to do in an activity, or know and be able to do at the end of a lesson or series of lessons. Compare *goal.*

pairwork: Activities done by two learners working together, e.g. question–answer pairwork.

passive vocabulary: Words only understood or recognized by learners, not used by them in their speech and writing. Contrast *active vocabulary.*

pattern: Grammatical sequence in which certain elements can be substituted; basis of drilling, e.g. *What about watching TV?*; What about *playing cards?* Also referred to as *structure.*

peer-correction: One learner correcting another. Compare *self-correction.*

peer observation: One teacher observing another's class.

PPP: Presentation-Practice-Production. Sequence of stages commonly used in introducing new language items. See also *presentation.*

presentation: First focus on new language items, intended to clarify form and *function.*

problem-solving: Task, usually done in pairs or groups, in which a problem has to be solved. Typically, it is goal-oriented and focuses on *communication*, not *pattern* or *structure.*

proficiency: Level of competence in English, e.g. a *proficiency test* may show whether a learner could manage to do a postgraduate course in the USA. Compare *achievement test.*

prompt: Assist a learner in completing something he or she is trying to say, e.g. when a learner has said 'My house is smaller . . . ' then stops, you could prompt with 'than . . . ' and a questioning gesture.

rapport: Positive relationship between teacher and learners.

realia: Real objects used as teaching aids.

review: Practice of previously encountered language.

reliability: Term used in *evaluation* and *testing*, e.g. a test would not be reliable if the questions had more than one correct answer, learners copied from one another, or teachers marked it in different ways. Compare *validity.*

remedial work: Work designed to help learners overcome gaps and *errors* in their English, especially *fossilized* errors.

role-play: Activity in which pairs or groups of learners act as different people, not themselves, e.g. doctor and patient, or customer and shop assistant. It is often combined with *simulation.*

scanning: Reading a text quickly to find specific information. Compare *skimming.*

scramble: Mix up parts of a text for learners to put in the correct order.

script: Basic text for a dialogue, *role-play*, or *simulation*, which learners may act out, and then modify. An unscripted role-play or simulation is totally improvised by the learners.

self-correction: Learner correcting him- or herself, perhaps assisted by the teacher. Compare *peer-correction.*

simulation: Activity in which pairs or groups of learners act out a situation, e.g. a visit to the doctor, or shopping. The learners may play themselves or *role-play* different people.

situation: Realistic context for communication, as in *role-play* and *simulation.*

skill: Each of the four major modes of communication–listening, speaking, reading, and writing.

skimming: Reading a text quickly to get the general idea or gist. Compare *scanning.*

slip: Mistake caused by factors such as tiredness or nerves. Compare *error.*

spelling pronunciation: Pronouncing words as the spelling seems to suggest.

structure: See *pattern.*

substitution practice: Getting the learners to produce many sentences of the same *pattern* with some elements changed, e.g. 'My *jacket* is about *two* years old'; 'My *watch* is about *five* years old'. *Drilling* often takes the form of substitution practice.

syllabus: plan or programme for a course, specifying content, sequence, and often methodology.

synonym: Word virtually the same in meaning as another word, e.g. 'little' is a synonym of 'small'. Compare *antonym*.

task: Activity which ends with a product or result, e.g. a poster or a solution to a problem.

technique: Way of doing a specific thing, e.g. an elicitation technique or a correction technique.

test/testing: Exercise or activity used to measure the learners' progress in a course, or their more general command of English; one possible element in *evaluation*. See also *achievement test, proficiency test*.

validity: Term in evaluation and testing, e.g. a test would not be valid if the exercises contained a large amount of language the learners had never encountered, and were quite different from the practice activities in the course. See also *construct validity, content validity*. Compare *reliability*.

wall-chart: Large picture or chart used as a teaching aid.

warm-up: Activity used at the beginning of a lesson to get the learners thinking and speaking in English.

whole-class: See *lockstep*.

SOURCES AND FURTHER READING

General background and methodology (Chapter 1)

All of the following books offer up-to-date views of teaching English:

Gower, R., D. Phillips, and S. Walters. 1995. *Teaching Practice Handbook (2nd edn.)*. Oxford: Heinemann.

Harmer, J. 1991. *The Practice of English Language Teaching (2nd edn.)*. Harlow: Longman.

Scrivener, J. 1994. *Learning Teaching*. Oxford: Heinemann.

Ur, P. 1996. *A Course in Language Teaching*. Cambridge: Cambridge University Press.

Creating conditions for foreign language learning (Chapter 1)

This topic is discussed in Harmer 1991; Scrivener 1994; Gower et al. 1995, and Ur 1996. The following books contain practical ideas as well as discussion of principles:

Atkinson, D. 1991. *Teaching Monolingual Classes*. Harlow: Longman.

Hadfield, J. 1992. *Classroom Dynamics*. Oxford: Oxford University Press.

Hughes, G. S. 1981. *A Handbook of Classroom English*. Oxford: Oxford University Press.

Willis, J. 1981. *Teaching English through English*. Harlow: Longman.

Presenting and practising new language items (Chapters 2 and 3)

This topic is discussed in Atkinson 1991; Harmer 1991; Scrivener 1994; Gower et al. 1995, and Ur 1996. Most of the following books contain practical ideas and specific teaching–learning activities as well as discussion of principles:

Byrne, D. 1986. *Teaching Oral English (2nd edn.)*. Harlow: Longman.

Byrne, D. 1988. *Teaching Writing Skills (2nd edn.)*. Harlow: Longman.

Edge, J. 1991. *Mistakes and Correction*. Harlow: Longman.

Harmer, J. 1989. *Teaching and Learning Grammar*. Harlow: Longman.

Kenworthy, J. 1987. *Teaching English Pronunciation*. Harlow: Longman.

Lee, W. 1980. *Language Teaching Games and Contests*. Oxford: Oxford University Press.

Littlewood, W. 1981. *Communicative Language Teaching*. Cambridge: Cambridge University Press.

Norrish, J. 1983. *Language Learners and their Errors*. London and Basingstoke: Macmillan.

Rinvolucri, M. 1985. *Grammar Games*. Cambridge: Cambridge University Press.

Swan, M. and **B. Smith.** 1987. *Learner English*. Cambridge: Cambridge University Press.

Ur, P. 1988. *Grammar Practice Activities*. Cambridge: Cambridge University Press.

Vocabulary work (Chapter 4)

Harmer 1991 has a good deal on this. The following books are exclusively on vocabulary, with background information and practical ideas:

Gairns, R. and **S. Redman.** 1986. *Working with Words*. Cambridge: Cambridge University Press.

Morgan, J. and **M. Rinvolucri.** 1986. *Vocabulary*. Oxford: Oxford University Press.

Developing communication skills (Chapters 5 and 6)

This topic is discussed in Littlewood 1981; Byrne 1986; Byrne 1988; Atkinson 1991; Harmer 1991; Scrivener 1994; Gower et al. 1995; Ur 1996. Most of the following books contain practical ideas and specific teaching–learning activities as well as discussion of principles:

Campbell, C. and **H. Kryszewska.** 1992. *Learner-based Teaching*. Oxford: Oxford University Press.

Hadfield, J. 1984. *Elementary Communication Games.* Walton-on-Thames: Nelson.

Hedge, T. 1988. *Writing.* Oxford: Oxford University Press.

Nuttal, C. 1996. *Teaching Reading Skills in a Foreign Language.* Oxford: Heinemann.

Porter-Ladousse, G. 1987. *Role Play.* Oxford: Oxford University Press.

Nolasco, R. and L. Arthur. 1987. *Conversation.* Oxford: Oxford University Press.

Seligson, P. 1997. *Helping Students to Speak.* London: Richmond.

Underwood, M. 1989. *Teaching Listening.* Harlow: Longman.

Ur, P. 1981. *Discussions that Work.* Cambridge: Cambridge University Press.

Ur, P. 1984. *Teaching Listening Comprehension.* Cambridge: Cambridge University Press.

Wallace, C. 1992. *Reading.* Oxford: Oxford University Press.

White, G. 1998. *Listening.* Oxford: Oxford University Press.

Williams, E. 1984. *Reading in the Language Classroom.* London and Basingstoke: Macmillan.

Wright, A., M. Buckby, and D. Betteridge. 1984. *Games for Language Learning.* Cambridge: Cambridge University Press.

Organizing review and remedial work (Chapter 7)

This is a neglected area, particularly from a practical angle. It is discussed in Gower et al. 1995, and in the books on treatment of errors (Norrish 1983; Edge 1991). For more theoretical background see:

Lightbown, P. and N. Spada. 1993. *How Languages are Learned.* Oxford: Oxford University Press.

Planning and managing classes (Chapter 8)

This topic is discussed in Harmer 1991; Hadfield 1992; Scrivener 1994; Gower et al. 1995, and Ur 1996. The following books deal with planning, class management, and teaching in different situations:

Brewster, J., G. Ellis, and D. Girard. 1992. *The Primary English Teacher's Guide.* Harmondsworth: Penguin.

Grundy, P. 1994. *Beginners.* Oxford: Oxford University Press.

Holme, R. 1996. *ESP Ideas*. Harlow: Longman.

Hutchinson, T. and A. Walters. 1987. *English for Specific Purposes*. Cambridge: Cambridge University Press.

Nolasco, R. and L. Arthur. 1988. *Large Classes*. London and Basingstoke: Macmillan.

Scott, W. and L. Ytreberg. 1990. *Teaching English to Children*. Harlow: Longman.

Tice, J. 1997. *The Mixed Ability Class*. London: Richmond.

Underwood, M. 1987. *Effective Class Management*. Harlow: Longman.

Working with a coursebook (Chapter 9)

This topic is discussed in Harmer 1991; Scrivener 1994; Gower et al. 1995, and Ur 1996. See also:

Grant, N. 1987. *Making the Most of your Textbook*. Harlow: Longman.

Teaching aids and materials (Chapter 10)

This topic is discussed in Harmer 1991; Gower et al. 1995; Scrivener 1994, and Ur 1996. See also:

Lonergan, J. 1984. *Video in Language Teaching*. Cambridge: Cambridge University Press.

Wright, A. and S. Haleem. 1991. *Visuals for the Language Classroom*. Harlow: Longman.

Testing and evaluation (Chapter 11)

This topic is discussed in Harmer 1991; Scrivener 1994; Gower et al. 1995, and Ur 1996. See also:

Heaton, J. B. 1990. *Classroom Testing*. Harlow: Longman.

Hughes, A. 1989. *Testing for Language Teachers*. Cambridge: Cambridge University Press.

Rea-Dickins, P. and K. Germaine. 1992. *Evaluation*. Oxford: Oxford University Press.

Approaches and developments in ELT (Chapter 12)

This topic is discussed in Harmer 1991, and specific developments in Hutchinson and Walters 1987. See also:

Dickinson, L. 1987. *Self-instruction in Language Learning.* Cambridge: Cambridge University Press.

Ellis, G. and **B. Sinclair.** 1989. *Learning to Learn English.* Cambridge: Cambridge University Press.

Howatt, A. P. R. 1984. *A History of English Language Teaching.* Oxford: Oxford University Press.

Lowes, R. and **Target, F.** 1998. *Helping Students to Learn.* London: Richmond.

Richards, J. C. and **T. S. Rodgers.** 1986. *Approaches and Methods in Language Teaching.* Cambridge: Cambridge University Press.

Willis, D. and **J. Willis** (eds.). 1996. *Challenge and Change in Language Teaching.* Oxford: Heinemann.

Continuing to develop as an EFL teacher (Chapter 12)

This topic is discussed in Scrivener 1994; Gower et al. 1995, and Ur 1996. See also:

Wajnryb, R. 1992. *Classroom Observation Tasks.* Cambridge: Cambridge University Press.

Language reference books

Teachers should have at least one good grammar book and one good dictionary. Here are some suggestions:

Grammar

Murphy, R. 1994. *English Grammar in Use.* Cambridge: Cambridge University Press.

Swan, M. 1995. *Practical English Usage (2nd edn.).* Oxford: Oxford University Press.

Collins COBUILD English Grammar. London and Glasgow: Collins.

Vocabulary

Collins COBUILD English Language Dictionary. London and Glasgow: Collins.

Longman Language Activator. Harlow: Longman.

Oxford Advanced Learner's Dictionary. Oxford: Oxford University Press.

You may also find a good bilingual dictionary very useful.

Teaching materials and activities

It is useful to collect coursebooks, other than the ones you are using, as a source of ideas. Another very useful source of ideas are teachers' resource books, for example, the 'Cambridge Handbooks for Language teachers' series (Cambridge University Press) and the 'Resource Books for Teachers' series (Oxford University Press).

INDEX

Entries relate to the introduction, chapters 1–12, the glossary, sources and further reading. g after the page number indicates terms described in the glossary.